USBORNE SCIENCE & EXPERIMENTS

WEATHER & CLIMATE

Fiona Watt and Francis Wilson, Television Weatherman

Edited by Corinne Stockley

Designed by Paul Greenleaf

Illustrated by Kuo Kang Chen, Peter Dennis and Denise Finney

Additional designs by Stephen Wright

Contents

First published in 1992 by Usborne Publishing Ltd, Usborne House, 83-85 Saffron Hill, London EC1N 8RT, England.

The name Usborne and the device 🐝 are Trade Marks of Usborne Publishing Ltd.

Universal Edition

Printed in Spain

About this book

From pleasant sunny days to devastating storms, the weather is part of daily life for everyone in the world. This book explains how many of the different elements of the atmosphere combine to produce different types of weather. It also describes how different weather conditions produce the wide variety of climates which are found throughout the world.

The book examines the ways in which the weather is monitored all over the world, and the processes involved in gathering information in order to make accurate forecasts. It explores how climates have changed since the Earth was first formed, and what effect current environmental problems may have on the atmosphere, weather and climates in the future.

Activities and projects

Special boxes like this one are used throughout the book for activities, projects and experiments. They will help you to understand the principles of different kinds of weather and its formation. You should be able to find most of the necessary equipment at home, but you may need to go to a hardware shop to buy a few of the items.

Using the glossary

The glossary on pages 46-47 is a useful reference point. It gives detailed explanations of the more complex terms used in the book, as well as introducing some new words.

This scene shows a tropical cyclone, or hurricane. Hurricane winds can cause serious damage to buildings and trees and also create gigantic waves which crash onto shores. To find out more about hurricanes and how they are formed, see pages 18-19.

Planetary weather

The Earth is one of a group of planets which make up the Solar System. Each planet is surrounded by a mixture of different gases which is called its atmosphere. The weather on each planet depends on its distance from the Sun and the movements of the gases in its atmosphere.

Mercury

The Sun

The Sun sends out energy in the form of rays of heat and light called radiation. The amount of heat and light energy which reaches the planets in the Solar System depends on their distance from the Sun.

The Sun's radiation

The Sun's radiation is made up of rays of different strengths of energy. Relatively speaking, they are all high energy rays but some are stronger than others. Some of these rays give us light, and they all heat up anything which absorbs them. Certain gases in the thermosphere and ozone in the stratosphere (see page 5) absorb some of the highest energy radiation (which is harmful). Clouds also absorb or reflect some of it. However, most of the Sun's radiation reaches the Earth's surface, where it is absorbed by the land or sea, or is reflected.

As it absorbs high energy radiation, the Earth warms up, and sends out lower energy radiation into the atmosphere Some of this radiation escapes into space, but some is absorbed by gases in the atmosphere, such as carbon dioxide. These gases then send out slightly lower energy radiation in all directions. Some of this reaches the Earth's surface where it is absorbed and again heats the surface.

High energy radiation from the Sun (solar radiation).

Most harmful radiation is absorbed by gases in the thermosphere and stratosphere (see page 5).

Some radiation is absorbed by, or reflected from clouds. Some is reflected from the Earth's surface (see page 7).

The warmed Earth gives off lower energy radiation. Some is absorbed by gases in the lowest layer of atmosphere.

These gases send out radiation in all directions.

Most of the high energy solar radiation is absorbed by the Earth's surface, which is heated.

Some radiation returns to the Earth's surface which again absorbs it and is heated.

Earth's surface

Weather on different planets

Scientists have used information from space probes to work out what the weather may be like on other planets. The atmosphere of each planet in the Solar System is held to the planet by gravity and pushes down on its surface. This is called atmospheric pressure (known as air pressure on Earth). The planets have different atmospheric gases and pressures, which greatly affect the weather found on each one. The examples below are the planets nearest to the Earth.

Venus

The Earth takes about 24 hours (a day) to rotate all the way round once.

Venus takes 243 Earth days to rotate.

Weather on Venus

On Venus, the atmosphere is very dense, with pressure over 90 times greater than on Earth. The planet's atmosphere is mainly made up of carbon dioxide, which is very good at trapping heat. This makes temperatures as high as 475°C (887°F).

Venus is surrounded by thick clouds containing droplets of sulphuric acid. These droplets may sometimes fall as rain, but they evaporate before reaching the ground and form clouds again. There are also continuous lightning storms.

The Earth

The Moon

The Moon

The Moon is not a planet, but a satellite of the Earth. A satellite is any object in space which travels around, or orbits, a larger object such as a planet. Other moons orbit other planets. Mars, for instance, has two moons, and Jupiter has sixteen.

There is no water, wind and weather on the Moon, and it is covered with dust. There is also no atmosphere surrounding it, because the Moon's force of gravity is so weak that any gases cannot be held to its surface.

Mars

The atmosphere on Mars is very thin with very low pressure. It is mainly made up of carbon dioxide with some nitrogen. There is no water on the surface, but there are areas of ice at the north and south poles. Temperatures are very low: -29°C (-20°F) during the day, falling to -85°C (-121°F) at night.

From Mars, the sky appears to be pink. This is caused by dust from the red, rocky surface being blown into the air by strong winds.

Jupiter

Jupiter's atmosphere appears to be a mass of swirling gases, which surround a solid centre, or core. The gases are thought to be hydrogen and helium. Temperatures on the planet are thought to be very low, not rising above -130°C (-200°F).

The Great Red Spot on the surface of Jupiter's atmosphere is thought to be a massive storm.

The Earth's atmosphere

The Earth's atmosphere is divided into layers (see below) according to temperature, although there are no solid boundaries separating each layer. The Earth is the only planet in the Solar System which has large amounts of water, both in its atmosphere, and on or below its surface.

The magnetosphere is the uppermost layer. It contains no gases, but forms a barrier which stops many particles from space entering the Earth's atmosphere. Most weather satellites (see page 25) are found way up beyond this layer.

The air in the exosphere is extremely thin as it contains very few gases. The top of this layer is about 900km (560 miles) from the ground. Some polar orbiting weather satellites (see page 25) are found in this layer.

The thermosphere contains gases which absorb some of the harmful solar radiation, and so heat up this layer. The temperature at the top, which is about 450km (280 miles) from the ground, may be as high as 2000°C (3632°F), but it decreases as you go down.

The mesosphere reaches a height of about 80km (50 miles). It is coldest at the top, about -100°C (-148°F), but warms up towards the bottom because of the warmer stratosphere below.

The top of the stratosphere is about 50km (31 miles) from the ground. Ozone gas forms a separate layer within it. This absorbs some of the Sun's harmful rays, heating up the layer. The temperature is highest at the top, about 0°C (32°F), cooling down towards the troposphere below. Jet aircraft fly here, where the air is still, or stable.

The troposphere varies in height between 10km (6 miles) and 20km (12 miles). Its lowest temperature is at the top, about -50°C (-58°F), but the air warms up the nearer you get to the surface. All the things which combine to make our weather are found in this layer.

Earth's surface

Heating the Earth

The way that the Sun's rays strike the surface of the Earth is important in determining the temperature of an area. In turn, the amount of heat received by any given area has a direct influence on the weather, as it affects the temperature of the air lying immediately above it.

The Sun's heat and the seasons

Not all places on the Earth's surface receive the same amount of heat from the Sun. The Earth is tilted at an angle, and its surface is curved, so the parallel rays of the Sun strike some areas full on, and others at more oblique angles.

As the Earth travels around the Sun in its orbit, the effect of its tilt is gradually to change the area which receives the most direct heat. At the start of each orbit, one hemisphere is tilted towards the Sun. After half the orbit (6 months later), the opposite hemisphere is in that position. The change in temperature due to this effect causes the seasons.

Near the equator, the seasons do not have great differences in temperature. The Sun's rays strike almost full-on all year round, so the temperature remains high.

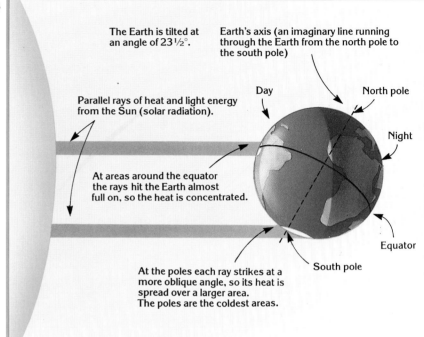

The Earth is tilted at an angle of 23½°.

Earth's axis (an imaginary line running through the Earth from the north pole to the south pole)

Parallel rays of heat and light energy from the Sun (solar radiation).

Day

North pole

Night

At areas around the equator the rays hit the Earth almost full on, so the heat is concentrated.

At the poles each ray strikes at a more oblique angle, so its heat is spread over a larger area. The poles are the coldest areas.

South pole

Equator

The further away from the equator a place is, the lower its summer and winter temperatures in comparison with places at the equator.

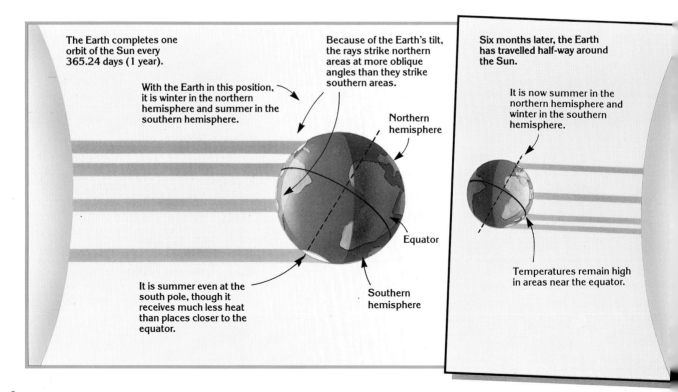

The Earth completes one orbit of the Sun every 365.24 days (1 year).

With the Earth in this position, it is winter in the northern hemisphere and summer in the southern hemisphere.

Because of the Earth's tilt, the rays strike northern areas at more oblique angles than they strike southern areas.

Northern hemisphere

Equator

It is summer even at the south pole, though it receives much less heat than places closer to the equator.

Southern hemisphere

Six months later, the Earth has travelled half-way around the Sun.

It is now summer in the northern hemisphere and winter in the southern hemisphere.

Temperatures remain high in areas near the equator.

Surface temperatures

As well as some places receiving more solar radiation than others, there are also differences in the amount of this radiation which is absorbed by different surfaces. Forests, sand and bare soil absorb more radiation than surfaces such as snow and ice, which reflect most of it. The temperature of the air in contact with a surface depends on the temperature of that surface.

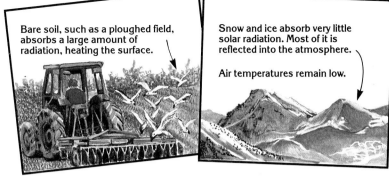

Bare soil, such as a ploughed field, absorbs a large amount of radiation, heating the surface.

Snow and ice absorb very little solar radiation. Most of it is reflected into the atmosphere.

Air temperatures remain low.

A bottle fountain

A bottle fountain shows how heated air expands. To make one, you will need a glass bottle with a plastic screw-top, a corkscrew, some food colouring, a straw, some sticky putty* and a needle.

What to do

1. Make a hole in the ▶ bottle top using a corkscrew (be careful with the sharp point).

Corkscrew

Bottle top

The hole must be big enough for the straw to fit through.

Food colouring

Bottle

Water

◀ 2. Half fill the bottle with cold water. Add a few drops of food colouring.

3. Screw the top tightly onto ▶ the bottle. Push the straw through the hole and seal around it with some sticky putty. Make a plug of sticky putty in the top of the straw. Use a needle to pierce a hole down through the plug.

Needle

Hole

Sticky putty

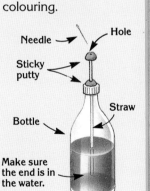

Straw

Bottle

Make sure the end is in the water.

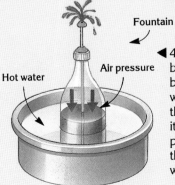

Fountain

Hot water

Air pressure

◀ 4. Carefully put the bottle in a deep bowl of very hot water. As the air in the bottle is heated, it expands and pushes down on the water, forcing water out of the straw.

Air temperatures

The Earth's surface is mainly heated by the absorption of solar radiation (see page 4). Where areas of the surface are warmer than the layer of air immediately above them, this air is heated.

Warmed air expands, becomes less dense and rises. Surrounding cooler air moves in to replace the rising warm air. The warm air cools as it rises, becomes denser again and eventually stops rising. It sinks back to Earth, where it may be heated again if the surface is still warmer than the air above. This circulation of warm and cold currents of air is called convection, and the currents are convection currents.

Air in contact with the surface is heated.

This air is less dense than the surrounding air, expands and rises.

Surrounding cooler air moves in to take its place.

The particles in warm air move around rapidly and are less densely packed.

Warm air eventually cools and sinks.

The particles in cool air move more slowly and are closer together, so this air is more dense.

Rising current of warm air (thermal)

Earth's surface

Convection currents can occur over large areas of the Earth's surface, where large masses of air are heated from below. They can also occur above a small, surface area, such as above a newly-ploughed field. The currents of rising warm air are called thermals.

* Sticky putty is used for sticking paper or posters to walls.

Pressure and winds

The pressure of the air on the Earth's surface is different in different places. This is partly due to the different amounts of heat they receive. Pressure differences cause the movement of air (winds).

Air pressure also decreases with altitude (height above sea level), because there is a greater amount of air pushing down on the surface at sea level than higher up, for instance on a mountain.

Differences in air pressure

When air rises, it leaves behind an area of lower pressure, because the upward-moving air is not pressing down so hard on the surface. Areas of high pressure are formed where air is sinking back down, and so pushing down harder.

If a pressure difference exists, air moves from the higher to the lower pressure area, in order to even out the pressure.

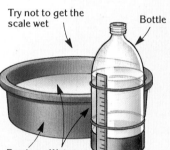

Rising air

The pressure drops at the surface as the air rises.

Air moves in from surrounding higher pressure areas.

Sinking air

The pressure increases at the surface as the air pushes down.

Surface air moves away towards surrounding lower pressure areas.

There are many areas of high and low pressure above the Earth's surface, due to such things as uneven surface heating. Air moves between these, forming surface winds.

Measuring air pressure

Air pressure is measured in millibars* on a barometer. You can make a model barometer using a large, narrow, plastic bottle, two rubber bands, some cardboard and some water.

What to do

1. Cut a 2.5cm (1in) strip of thin cardboard and draw a scale along one edge. Attach the cardboard to the bottle using the rubber bands.

Bottle

Thin cardboard

Rubber bands

Scale

Try not to get the scale wet

Bottle

Bowl   Water

2. Fill the bottle with water so it is three quarters full. Also fill the bowl nearly to the top with water.

3. Place your hand over the top of the bottle and turn it upside-down. Put your hand into the bowl so that the neck of the bottle is under the water. Remove your hand from under the bottle and stand it in the bowl.

Turn the bottle over carefully.

Try not to let any water out.

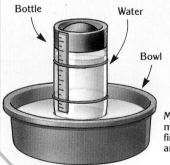

Bottle   Water

Bowl

4. The water level in the bottle will rise and fall with the air pressure, as more or less air pushes down on the water in the bowl.

Mark the water level on the day you make your barometer (you could find out what the air pressure is, and write this too).

Major pressure areas of the world

Around the Earth there are several major bands where high or low pressure predominates (although in each band individual areas of different pressure may occur – see page 10). There is a general pattern of air movement from the high pressure to the low pressure areas.

The Earth's surface receives the most solar radiation around the equator. The land greatly heats up the air immediately above it, and this vast amount of air rises, leaving a band of predominately low pressure, called the Intertropical Convergence Zone (ITCZ), at the surface. This sets up all other air movements.

The warm air rising above the equator spreads out and cools, sinking around latitudes 30° north and south of the equator. The sinking air pushes down on the surface, creating a band of high pressure, so when it reaches the surface, the air moves north and south towards areas of lower pressure.

The general movement of air around the world

North pole (90°N)

High pressure

Low pressure   60°N

High pressure   30°N

Lines of latitude (imaginary lines parallel to the equator).

They are measured in degrees and are used on maps to show distance north or south of the equator.

Heated air rises and moves towards the poles.

Low pressure (ITCZ)   Equator (0°)

The air moving towards the equator forms the trade winds (see winds, below right).

Air cools and sinks.

High pressure   30°S

Low pressure   60°S

Warm air collides with polar air and rises.

South pole (90°S)

Cold polar air

This movement of air at the surface forms the polar winds (see right).

Air cools and sinks.

High pressure

At about 60°N and 60°S, cold air moving away from the poles meets the warmer air from nearer the equator. The warmer air is less dense and is forced to rise, forming areas of low pressure at the surface. This air cools and sinks again around the poles, forming a band of high pressure.

The Coriolis effect

When air moves from high pressure to low pressure, the winds do not take the most direct possible route. They "try" to, but are deflected sideways. This is due to the rotating movement of the Earth, and is called the Coriolis effect.

The forces involved have the effect of deflecting the winds in the northern hemisphere to the right of their "intended" direction, and those in the southern hemisphere to the left. The Coriolis effect acts on the world's main air movements (see left) to determine the directions of the world's main winds.

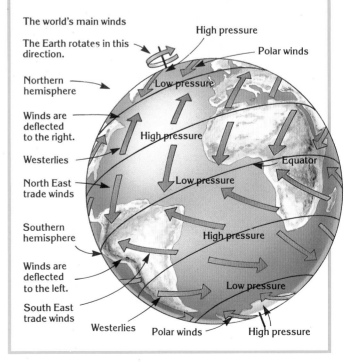

The world's main winds

The Earth rotates in this direction.

High pressure

Polar winds

Northern hemisphere

Low pressure

Winds are deflected to the right.

High pressure

Westerlies

North East trade winds

Low pressure

Equator

Southern hemisphere

High pressure

Winds are deflected to the left.

Low pressure

South East trade winds

Westerlies   Polar winds   High pressure

Moving air

The air around the world is on the move all the time. The main high and low pressure bands (see page 9) set up the general, long-term pattern of air movements. However, individual, small or very large high and low pressure areas are also constantly being created over different places on the surface. This causes surface movements of air (winds) between them. On any particular day, these may blow in a different, even opposing, direction to the main, general movement of the air.

Pressure differences

The creation of different highs and lows in different places is mainly due to fast high-level winds which blow around the Earth in the direction of its spin (from west to east). The strongest ones travel around at high levels roughly above 60°N and 60°S where the high level polar air is met by warmer air (see page 9). There are also weaker ones at 30°N and 30°S.

The strong winds follow wavy paths, formed because the warmer air makes more progress towards the pole over some areas than others. The winds travel fastest where the warm air pushes the greatest distance into the polar air, so they have uneven speeds, slowing down and speeding up as they travel. At their fastest they are called jet streams.

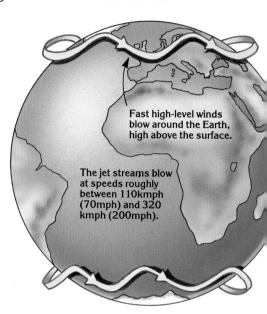

Fast high-level winds blow around the Earth, high above the surface.

The jet streams blow at speeds roughly between 110kmph (70mph) and 320 kmph (200mph).

The wavy paths (see below) and uneven speeds of the winds disrupt the air around and below them. In some areas, the air gets squashed together, so some gets pushed down, creating higher pressure at the surface. In others, the air thins out, so underlying air moves up to to fill up the space, creating lower surface pressure.

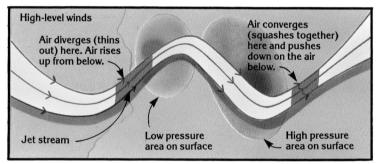

High-level winds

Air diverges (thins out) here. Air rises up from below.

Air converges (squashes together) here and pushes down on the air below.

Jet stream

Low pressure area on surface

High pressure area on surface

Because the air is disrupted, low pressure areas may form in a general high pressure band, and vice versa. The air which then moves in or away to even up the pressure may move in a different direction to the general pattern. This is because these closer pressure differences have the strongest influence.

All these air movements have a "knock-on" effect. Air becomes disrupted elsewhere, and this leads to the irregular day-to-day pattern of air movements around the globe.

Moving areas of pressure

Surface winds are always blowing from the centres of high pressure areas towards the centres of low pressure ones, but, in addition, these centres themselves are also moving. Having been created over one particular place on the Earth's surface, they are moved around by the high-level winds above them.

As the centres move, they influence each other. The closer they are, the greater this influence. If the pressure difference between a high pressure centre and its surroundings is not that great, the air moving out of the high does not move very fast. So high pressure areas, with no other influences, have slow surface winds.

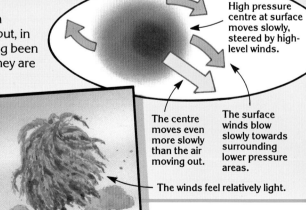

High pressure centre at surface moves slowly, steered by high-level winds.

The centre moves even more slowly than the air moving out.

The surface winds blow slowly towards surrounding lower pressure areas.

The winds feel relatively light.

Temperature and humidity

A mass of air may be warmer or colder, drier or more humid (contain more water vapour) than the air in the area it moves into. If so, it will bring a change of weather with it. Its characteristics depend on where it has come from and the type of surface it has travelled over, but also on its speed. Slow-moving air has more time to be affected by the surfaces it passes over.

Air temperature is influenced by surface temperatures. At places such as the poles and the equator, these are obviously very different, but they may also differ in areas which are quite close. One reason for this may be the different types of land which the Sun's rays fall on (see page 7), another that the areas are land and sea. At different times (in a daily cycle or a longer seasonal one), the sea may be warmer than the land, or vice versa.

Land heats up quickly, because just the surface is heated.

Sun heats land only to a shallow depth.

This means it cools down quickly as well.

Sea heats up more slowly, because it is heated to a greater depth.

Sun heats surface water.

The waves travel in a circular pattern, moving the heated water away from the surface.

Lower layers of the water are heated.

Because of this, it stores heat for longer and cools down more slowly.

The humidity of a mass of air is greater if it is travelling over the sea, as water evaporates from the sea into the air. Air which has travelled far over land tends to contain little water vapour.

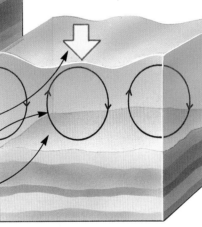

If a high pressure centre is close to a low pressure centre, though, the pressure difference between the two areas is more acute, and the air moves faster. The larger the pressure difference, the faster the air will move, so the stronger the surface winds.

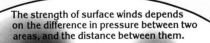

The strength of surface winds depends on the difference in pressure between two areas, and the distance between them.

High pressure area

Low pressure area

The closer two areas of different pressures are, the faster the winds will blow between them.

Strong winds mean a large pressure difference. The air moves to even it out.

Classifying air masses

Air masses are classified according to the area they originally came from, called their source.

Air masses which form over seas and oceans are called maritime (m) air masses.

A tropical maritime (mT) air mass develops over warm seas. It is warm and moist.

A polar maritime (mP) air mass forms over the sea near the poles. It is cold and moist.

Continental (c) air masses form over land.

A tropical continental (cT) air mass develops over hot, dry land. It is warm and dry.

Polar continental (cP) air masses develop over land near the poles. They are cold and dry.

Clouds

Clouds are made up of millions of tiny droplets of water or ice crystals, formed when air is cooled. Clouds are formed in several ways and are named according to their shape, height and size. They help to forecast the type of weather which may follow. They are often associated with precipitation (rain, snow, sleet or hail), but not all clouds lead to this kind of weather.

Water vapour

Water is found in the air as an invisible gas called water vapour. This is formed when water in rivers, lakes, seas and oceans is heated. The heat makes the water evaporate (turn into vapour), and it rises into the air. The humidity of the air is the amount of water vapour it contains.

The humidity of the air varies from place to place and with temperature. When air can hold no more water vapour it is said to be saturated.

The very hot air in tropical areas (see pages 32-33) often holds a large amount of water vapour.

The air here is said to be very humid or "sticky".

How clouds are formed

Air contains millions of microscopic particles of dust. When moist air rises, expands and cools, any water vapour it contains condenses (turns back into a liquid) onto the surface of the particles. This forms minute water droplets which group together to make clouds. The temperature at which this happens is called the dew point. If the cloud temperature falls below freezing, the water droplets freeze to form ice crystals.

There are several reasons why air rises and clouds are formed.

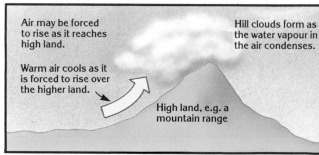

Air may be forced to rise as it reaches high land.

Hill clouds form as the water vapour in the air condenses.

Warm air cools as it is forced to rise over the higher land.

High land, e.g. a mountain range

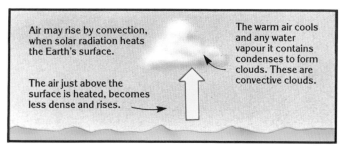

Air may rise by convection, when solar radiation heats the Earth's surface.

The warm air cools and any water vapour it contains condenses to form clouds. These are convective clouds.

The air just above the surface is heated, becomes less dense and rises.

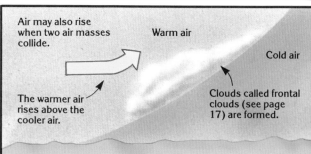

Air may also rise when two air masses collide.

Warm air

Cold air

The warmer air rises above the cooler air.

Clouds called frontal clouds (see page 17) are formed.

Making a "cloud"

This experiment shows how clouds are formed as warm air is cooled. You will need a large glass jar, a small metal baking tray and some ice.

What to do
1. Pour 2.5cm (1in) of hot water into the jar.

2. Place some ice cubes in the baking tray and put the tray on top of the jar.

3. As the air inside the jar rises and is cooled by the ice, the water vapour it contains condenses into droplets.

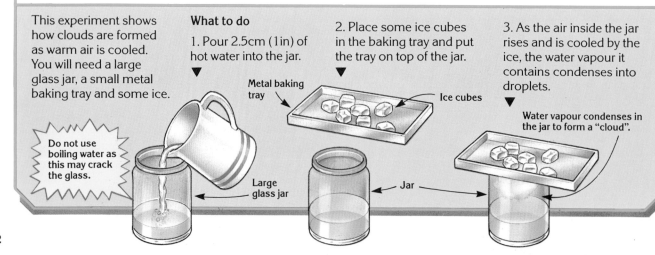

Do not use boiling water as this may crack the glass.

Metal baking tray

Ice cubes

Water vapour condenses in the jar to form a "cloud".

Large glass jar

Jar

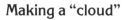

The main cloud types

The main types of cloud are recognized by their shape and height. There are three main cloud types called cirrus, cumulus and stratus. There are many combinations of these clouds and different types may exist in the sky at the same time.

Cirrus clouds are high level clouds, usually found above 6000m (20,000ft). They are made up of ice crystals and have a feathery, wispy appearance.

Cumulus clouds are found at different heights. They are individual, rounded clouds with fairly flat bases. They are often seen on dry, sunny days.

Stratus clouds form a layer or sheet across the sky. They are found at low levels, below 500m (1,650ft) and often produce light rain and drizzle.

Many different cloud patterns are formed from combinations of the main cloud types. Their names refer to the types of clouds or the height at which they are found. For instance, the word 'alto' in a cloud type indicates that the clouds are middle level clouds, found between 2000m and 6000m (6,500ft and 20,000ft). Stratus means layered, and nimbus indicates rain or snow is falling from the cloud.

Cumulonimbus clouds are like massive cumulus clouds. They have flat tops and may extend to great heights. They are associated with heavy rain and thunder (see page 18).

Cirrus clouds

Cirrostratus clouds are cirrus clouds which form a thin, almost transparent, layer over the whole sky. They often bring rain.

Cirrocumulus are a combination of cirrus and cumulus clouds. They are individual clouds of ice which are sometimes arranged in rows.

Altostratus clouds normally form a grey sheet of cloud across the sky. Sunlight can usually be seen filtering through this.

Altocumulus are small grey or white cumulus clouds of roughly the same size, often lying in rows and sometimes joined together.

Nimbostratus clouds are a thick layer of grey clouds with an uneven base, which blot out the Sun completely.

Stratocumulus clouds form a sheet of rounded cumulus clouds which are almost joined together.

Cumulus clouds

Stratus clouds

Measuring cloud cover

The number of clouds covering the sky is measured in oktas. The number of oktas indicates how much of the sky is covered by clouds. Oktas are measured on a scale of 0 to 8 (8 oktas means that the sky is completely covered). For example, a weather forecaster may describe the sky as having four oktas of cloud, which means that half the sky is obscured by clouds.

A sky with 3 oktas of cumulus cloud.

Aircraft trails are artificial cirrus clouds made up of ice crystals.

Aircraft trails

High-flying aircraft sometimes leave a white trail behind them when the air is very cold. The aircraft's exhaust system sends out a mixture of hot gases, containing large amounts of water vapour. The water vapour cools, condenses and freezes in the cold air, forming thin "cloud" trails. These are called contrails.

13

Water in the air

Water is found in the air as water vapour or as water droplets and ice crystals in clouds (see page 12), depending on the temperature of the air. The temperature of the air also determines the type of precipitation (rain, snow, sleet or hail) which may fall from the clouds.

Rain and snow

The temperature of the air in clouds determines the way that rain and snow are formed. In areas such as tropical areas, where the cloud temperature is mainly above the freezing point of 0°C (32°F), rain is formed by a process called coalescence. The clouds are made up of millions of minute droplets of water and as these droplets collide, they join together, forming larger droplets.

Gradually the droplets increase in size until they are too heavy to be kept up in the cloud by air currents and fall as raindrops.

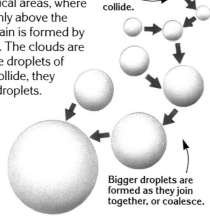

Microscopic droplets in clouds collide.

Bigger droplets are formed as they join together, or coalesce.

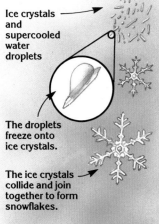

Ice crystals and supercooled water droplets

The droplets freeze onto ice crystals.

The ice crystals collide and join together to form snowflakes.

Scientists think that the shape of snowflakes depends on the height and temperature at which they are formed.

In cooler areas, clouds may stretch up into air which is below freezing. These clouds are a mixture of water droplets, lower down, and ice crystals and special supercooled water droplets higher up. These droplets exist as water even though the temperature is below freezing.

As well as coalescence at the bottom, a process called accretion happens higher up in these clouds. The ice crystals attract the supercooled droplets, which freeze onto them. As the crystals grow and stick to others, snowflakes form. When they become too heavy to be held up, they fall.

In areas where the air temperature near the ground remains below freezing, snow falls, but if the temperature is above freezing, the flakes melt and fall as rain. Sleet is a mixture of snowflakes and raindrops.

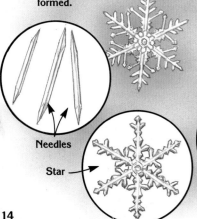

Needles

Star

Plates

Hail

Hail forms in cumulonimbus clouds (see page 13), which have strong upward and downward currents of air moving within them. The temperature at the top of these clouds is well below freezing. As ice crystals rush around the cloud, they collide with supercooled water droplets and are rapidly coated with layers of ice.

More ice layers are added as the hailstones are swept up and down and tossed about in the cloud. They eventually fall when they are too heavy to be held up by the air currents within the cloud.

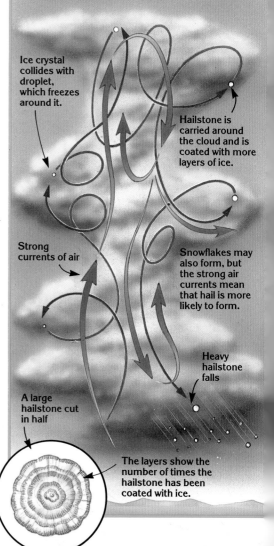

Ice crystal collides with droplet, which freezes around it.

Hailstone is carried around the cloud and is coated with more layers of ice.

Strong currents of air

Snowflakes may also form, but the strong air currents mean that hail is more likely to form.

Heavy hailstone falls

A large hailstone cut in half

The layers show the number of times the hailstone has been coated with ice.

Mist and fog

Mist and fog are "surface clouds", made up of minute droplets of water. Like clouds, they are formed when water vapour in the air condenses as it cools below its dew point. Clouds form when air is cooled as it rises, whereas fog forms when a deep layer of air is cooled by the underlying surface. Sea fog is formed when warm, moist air is cooled over a cold sea (see page 22).

The difference between mist and fog is determined by the density of the "cloud". This affects the distance which can be seen ahead, or the visibility. Fog is more dense, resulting in poorer visibility than in mist (see page 27).

The surface is cooler than the air.

Water vapour condenses.

Fog forms above the surface.

Dew

Dew forms when air immediately in contact with a cold surface is cooled to its dew point. The water vapour condenses into dew droplets on the surface. Dew is always found when there is fog, but it may also form on a clear night when the layer of air touching the surface reaches its dew point, but the air immediately above does not.

Air directly in contact with surface cools below its dew point.

Water vapour condenses into droplets of dew on cold surfaces.

Measuring rainfall

The amount of rain or snow which falls can be measured on a rain gauge. To make a rain gauge you will need a tall plastic bottle (with a flat, clear bottom) and a ruler.

What to do

1. Use a sharp pair of scissors to carefully cut around the plastic bottle, about 10cm (4in) from the top.

No lid

Plastic bottle

Scissors

Flat, clear bottom

Top piece or funnel

◄ 2. Fit the top piece of the bottle upside-down in the bottom piece. These form the funnel and collecting jar. The funnel directs rain into the collecting jar and also forms a barrier to stop any of it evaporating.

Bottom piece or collecting jar

Rain gauge

Remember to empty the rain gauge after each measurement.

3. Sink the base of the bottle in the ground in an ▶ open area, away from trees and buildings. Use a ruler to measure the amount of rain which falls in a given time. You could make a daily record.

Ground

If you are measuring snow, you may not need the funnel. About 12cm (4½in) = 1cm (⅓in) of water.

Frost

Frost occurs when the ground temperature is below freezing. The most common type is known as hoar frost. It is made up of tiny ice crystals. Some of these are frozen dew, others form when water vapour turns directly into ice as it comes into contact with a freezing surface. This happens without the water vapour passing through the stage of condensing into water droplets (dew).

On a cold winter morning, white hoar frost is often seen covering the ground.

The ground may freeze (a ground frost) without there being any white covering, if there is not enough moisture in the air.

15

Highs, lows and fronts

Areas of high and low pressure are constantly moving across the Earth's surface, with air moving between them (see pages 10-11). Air moving into an area brings with it the characteristics of where it has come from. Where two air masses with different characteristics meet, the air does not mix easily, but forms a boundary, called a front.

Movement of air around highs and lows

Meteorologists refer to areas of high pressure as highs or anticyclones, and areas of low pressure as lows, depressions or cyclones.

As surface winds blow into a low, and away from a high, the Coriolis effect (see page 9) makes them circulate around the pressure centre.

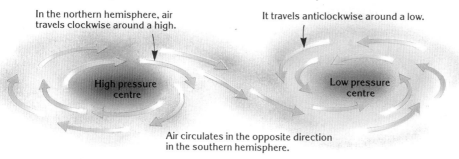

In the northern hemisphere, air travels clockwise around a high.

It travels anticlockwise around a low.

High pressure centre

Low pressure centre

Air circulates in the opposite direction in the southern hemisphere.

Highs and lows on a weather map

Weather maps (see page 28) show air pressure readings at sea level. On these maps, places of equal pressure are joined by lines called isobars. Surface winds do not blow from high to low pressure directly across the isobars. Instead, they blow almost parallel to the isobars. This is because the air spirals into and out of the high and low pressure centres (see above).

The average pressure of the atmosphere has been set as 1013mb (29.91psi)*. However, areas are not marked as high or low in relation to this, but in relation to the pressure in surrounding areas. For instance, a pressure of 1008mb is marked as a low when the surrounding areas are 1032mb, but as a high when the surrounding areas have readings of 996mb.

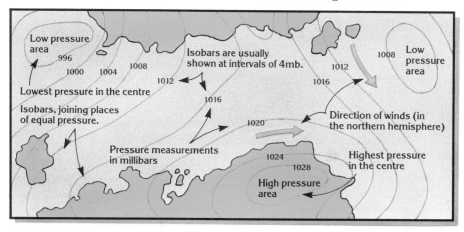

Low pressure area
996
1000 1004 1008

Isobars are usually shown at intervals of 4mb.

1012
1016

Low pressure area

1008
1012
1016

Lowest pressure in the centre

Isobars, joining places of equal pressure.

Pressure measurements in millibars

1020

Direction of winds (in the northern hemisphere)

1024
1028

Highest pressure in the centre

High pressure area

The Buys-Ballot law

The Buys-Ballot law states that in the northern hemisphere, if you have your back to the wind, there will be lower pressure on your left and higher on your right. In the southern hemisphere, low pressure is found on the right.

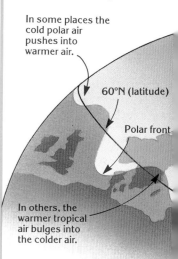

Fronts

A front is the boundary between two masses of moving air with different temperatures and humidity. The main front is called the polar front and is found around latitudes 60°N and 60°S, where cold polar air meets warmer tropical air coming from towards the equator. In some places along the polar front, the warm air mass bulges into the cold air and in others the cold air pushes out into the warm air. This is because there are uneven pressure differences along the front.

In some places the cold polar air pushes into warmer air.

60°N (latitude)

Polar front

In others, the warmer tropical air bulges into the colder air.

In general along the front, the warm air rises over the cooler air. It rises at different speeds in different places, forming areas of low pressure. The greater the temperature difference between the warm and cold air, the faster the warm air will rise. The greatest differences in temperature occur at the points where one mass of air has pushed furthest into the other. High-level winds (see page 10) may also be causing air to rise in certain places, speeding it up even more.

* mb = millibars, psi = pounds per square inch. To convert millibars to pounds per square inch, multiply by 0.02953.

Fronts and pressure

Wherever air is rising along the polar front, there is a fall in pressure. However, individual centres of low pressure are formed where the air is rising most quickly as these are the points which have the lowest pressure compared with those on either side of them. Because of these individual centres, the polar front is never seen as a continuous line, but as a series of individual fronts, occurring at the low pressure centres. These are known as frontal depressions. The surrounding warm and cold air moves towards them, because they have the lowest pressure. Winds do not blow directly into areas of low pressure, though, (see page 16), so the air circulates around them as it moves in.

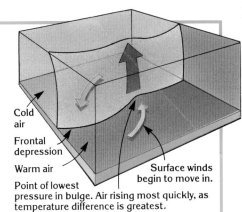

Cold air

Frontal depression

Warm air

Point of lowest pressure in bulge. Air rising most quickly, as temperature difference is greatest.

Surface winds begin to move in.

Warm and cold fronts

As the winds circulate around a frontal depression, they bring warm air into an area where there is colder air, and vice versa. This movement of air forms warm and cold fronts (as shown in the diagram below).

Where cooler air moves into a warmer area, it is known as a cold front. The cool air pushes under the warm air, forcing it to rise.

Where warm air advances into an area to replace cooler air, it is known as a warm front. The warm air rides up over the cooler air.

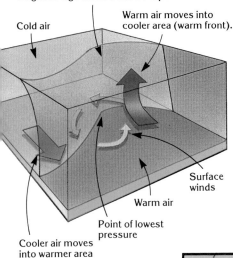

Original bulge forms a wave shape.

Cold air

Warm air moves into cooler area (warm front).

Surface winds

Warm air

Point of lowest pressure

Cooler air moves into warmer area (cold front).

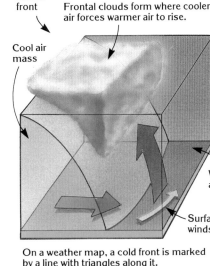

A cold front

Frontal clouds form where cooler air forces warmer air to rise.

Cool air mass

Warmer air mass

Surface winds

On a weather map, a cold front is marked by a line with triangles along it.

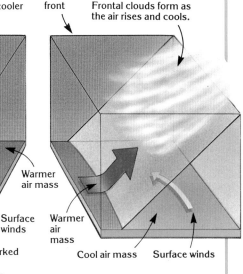

A warm front

Frontal clouds form as the air rises and cools.

Warmer air mass

Cool air mass

Surface winds

A warm front is marked by a line with semicircles along it.

Occluded fronts

A cold front gradually moves towards a warm front and may eventually catch it up. If it does so, it undercuts the warm air and lifts it right off the ground. The front is then described as an occluded front. This extra "push", as the cold air moves in and lifts the warm air, can produce huge clouds and very heavy rain.

Occluded fronts on weather maps are lines with both semicircles and triangles.

Changing weather

Like all pressure areas, frontal depressions are not stationary, but are moved by high-level winds. They bring a general pattern of unsettled weather to places they pass over. Cirrus clouds are usually the first sign that a depression may be approaching, followed by a sequence of other clouds and rain. However, no two depressions produce exactly the same sequence of weather.

Thunderstorms and hurricanes

Storms are a combination of strong winds and heavy rain, snow or hail, and form in low pressure areas. Under certain conditions, minor storms can develop into thunderstorms or hurricanes, which can cause much damage to areas where they occur.

Thunderstorms

Thunderstorms form when particularly warm, moist air rises into cold air above land or sea. As the humid air rises to a great height, water vapour condenses, forming huge cumulonimbus clouds.

Water droplets and ice crystals in the clouds bump together and break up as they rub against each other in strong currents of air. This action builds up positive electrical charges at the top of the clouds and negative charges at the base.

When the charge at the base of the cloud gets to a certain strength, electrical energy is released and passes through the air to another point with the opposite charge, such as the ground. This release of energy is called the leader stroke and forms a path of charged air for the main stroke to travel along. The main stroke travels back up to the cloud and produces a flash of lightning.

At the same time as the main stroke travels up, it heats the air, causing it to expand very quickly. This expansion of air produces the sound we hear as thunder.

Cumulonimbus cloud

Leader stroke forms a charged path.

Main stroke follows path back up to cloud and produces a flash of lightning.

The air expands very quickly, producing thunder.

If the storm is directly overhead, the thunder will be heard at the same time as the lightning is seen.

If not, the lightning is seen several seconds before the thunder is heard, as the speed of light is faster than the speed of sound.

Thunderstorms die out once the charges in the clouds have evened out.

Hurricanes

In tropical areas, thunderstorms may develop into violent storms with torrential rain, and wind speeds reaching as much as 300km per hour (186mph). Meteorologists call these storms tropical cyclones, but they are more commonly known as hurricanes. They are also given other names in different countries around the world, such as typhoons in S.E. Asia and willy-willies in Australia.

Hurricanes form only above tropical seas between the latitudes 5° and 20° north and south of the equator, where the sea temperature is above 27°C (80°F), and so the conditions of heat and moisture are at their most extreme.

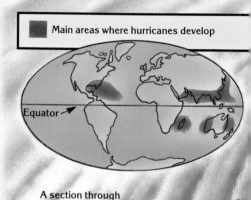

Main areas where hurricanes develop

Equator

A section through a hurricane

Rings of cumulonimbus clouds form around a hurricane's centre. They join at the top, which may reach the top of the troposphere (see page 5).

A hurricane may have a diameter of 500km (300 miles), covering a much greater area than a thunderstorm.

Thunder and lightning often occur during hurricanes.

The development of a hurricane

It is not fully understood why a hurricane develops, as moist air is always rising above warm seas, but it is thought that an "extra" low pressure area moving in over the sea may set them off.

As the pressure falls rapidly, strong surface winds area formed as air is sucked in towards the centre of the low. At the centre, the air speeds up and spirals upwards. Vast quantities of water vapour in the rising air condense to form massive cumulonimbus clouds. As the water vapour condenses, enormous amounts of heat are given out which makes the air rise even faster, and in turn increases the speed of the surface winds moving in.

Naming hurricanes

Lists of alternate male and·female names are drawn up each year. As soon as a storm becomes hurricane strength with wind speeds over 199km/h (74mph), it is given the next name on the list.

Hurricane Gilbert in 1988 caused severe damage to islands in the Caribbean.

Air at the centre rises rapidly, forming a spiralling column.

As the vapour condenses, heat is given off, making the air rise faster.

The eye of the storm

Down the centre of the storm there is a column of air 30-50km (20-30 miles) wide, called the eye. The air here is slowly sinking and the winds are light. As the eye passes overhead, the wind and the rain stop for a short time, only to start again as the other side of the hurricane passes over.

Strong surface winds

Warm sea

Tracking hurricanes

Like all storms, hurricanes do not stay in one place, but travel away from the area where they form. Their path is influenced by the movements of high-level winds (see page 10) and the direction of warm sea currents. A hurricane dies out when it reaches an area where there is no longer the necessary warmth and moisture, such as when it reaches a cool sea, or land.

Satellite images are used to detect where a storm may develop into a hurricane.

Meteorologists try to predict the path which a hurricane may take, and issue warnings to people who are at risk from the storm.

A satellite image of a hurricane

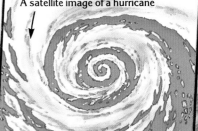

Extreme weather conditions

Extreme weather conditions, such as floods or droughts, sometimes interrupt the usual pattern of weather in some areas. In other places, extreme conditions are experienced each year as part of the seasonal pattern.

Droughts

A drought occurs when there is less than 0.2mm (¹⁄₁₀₀in) of rain, or other type of precipitation, over a period of at least fifteen days. Droughts may occur because of a high blocking the passage of rain-bearing lows across an area (see page 21). They also occur when areas of land are cleared of vegetation in areas which are already very dry (see pictures, right).

Water vapour is given off by plants.

Moist air rises and cools, and clouds form, which may give rain.

Where there are few plants to feed many animals, they are all eaten, leaving the ground bare. This is called overgrazing.

There are no plants to give off water vapour, so no clouds form as the rising air is dry.

Flooding

Flooding may occur for several reasons, for instance, if large amounts of rain fall and there is too much water to drain away. Flooding also occurs when sea levels rise, when the land is swamped by waves caused by storms, or when snow on land melts as temperatures rise rapidly, causing rivers to overflow.

When more than 15mm (⁶⁄₁₀in) of rain falls in 3 hours, meteorologists describe the conditions as a "flash flood".

When a flash flood occurs, there is too much water to drain away. It flows rapidly across the surface, flooding areas in its path.

Monsoons

The term monsoon describes winds which blow, in tropical areas such as India and S.E. Asia, from roughly opposite directions in different seasons. The combination of the extremes of temperature and pressure in these areas, and the position of the land and the sea, produces extreme weather conditions.

This scene shows the extremely heavy rain which falls during the wet monsoon season.

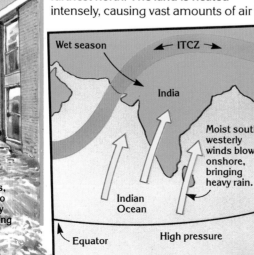

One of the two winds is dry, while the other brings extremely heavy rain, so there is a dry monsoon, which creates a dry season, and a wet one which brings a rainy season.

For example, in India, the wet monsoon blows when the Sun lies almost directly overhead, and the equatorial band of low pressure, called the ITCZ (see page 9) is furthest north. The land is heated intensely, causing vast amounts of air to rise, forming even lower pressure on the surface. Very moist winds blow in from the Indian Ocean, to replace the rising air. Many places receive as much as 3,000mm (118in) of rain during the rainy season.

The dry season occurs when the sun is no longer directly overhead and the ITCZ is furthest south. This low pressure zone causes winds to blow from high pressure over the land towards the ITCZ. These winds are dry as they have travelled a large distance over the land.

Wet season
ITCZ
India
Moist south-westerly winds blow onshore, bringing heavy rain.
Indian Ocean
Equator
High pressure

Dry season
High pressure
Dry north-easterly winds
ITCZ

Measuring air humidity

During the wet monsoon, the humidity of the air (see page 12) is extremely high. Humidity is sometimes measured on wet and dry bulb thermometers. To make these you will need two thermometers, with scales roughly ranging from 0°C to 35°C (32°F to 95°F), some cotton wool, two rubber bands and a small bowl of water.

What to do

1. Wrap the bulb end ▶ of each thermometer in equal amounts of cotton wool. Secure each piece with a rubber band.

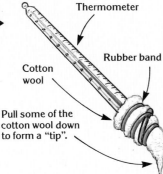

Thermometer

Rubber band

Cotton wool

Pull some of the cotton wool down to form a "tip".

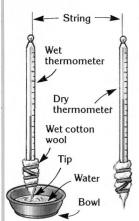

String

Wet thermometer

Dry thermometer

Wet cotton wool

Tip

Water

Bowl

◀ 2. Stick a piece of thin string to the other end of each thermometer. Use drawing pins to hang the thermometers outside in the shade. Put a bowl of water below one of the thermometers so that its tip is in the water.

3. After 30 minutes, read each thermometer. Work out the difference between the two temperatures. Use the chart to calculate the humidity of the air.

Heat is given off as water evaporates from the cotton wool, so the temperature shown on the wet thermometer will be lower than that on the dry one. If the air contains large amounts of water vapour, less water evaporates, so the temperature difference between the thermometers will be smaller, and the humidity measurement higher.

Humidity is measured as a percentage. 100% humidity is very humid and the air feels sticky.

Temperature on the dry thermometer ▼	Difference between wet and dry bulb thermometers ▼									
	1°C 2°F	2°C 3°F	3°C 5°F	4°C 7°F	5°C 9°F	6°C 11°F	7°C 13°F	8°C 14°F	9°C 16°F	10°C 18°F
10-14°C (50-57°F)	85	75	60	50	40	30	15	5	0	0
15-19°C (59-66°F)	90	80	65	60	50	40	30	20	10	5
20-25°C (68-77°F)	90	80	70	65	55	45	40	30	25	20

Humidity (%) ◀

Blocking highs

Areas around 60° north and south of the equator usually experience changeable weather as areas of high and low pressure are moved across them by the high-level winds (see page 10). The wavy pattern of these winds, and the position of the waves, changes frequently, bringing highs and lows which change the weather.

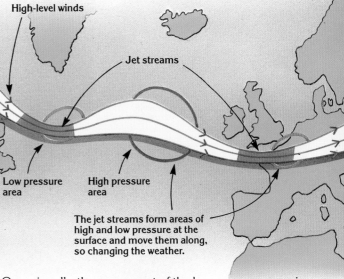

High-level winds

Jet streams

Low pressure area

High pressure area

The jet streams form areas of high and low pressure at the surface and move them along, so changing the weather.

Occasionally, the movement of the low pressure areas is "blocked" by an area of high pressure which remains in one place for a long period of time and prevents any change in the weather for several days or weeks. These areas of high pressure are known as blocking highs.

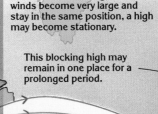

If the waves in the high-level winds become very large and stay in the same position, a high may become stationary.

This blocking high may remain in one place for a prolonged period.

The weather in the area of the blocking high remains very settled for a long period.

It diverts the flow of the high-level winds, and the lows are steered around it.

Other areas experience unsettled weather because of these diverted lows.

Blocking highs can persist for several days or even weeks. They may produce prolonged cold weather, with ice and snow in winter, or very hot, dry weather in summer, which may lead to a drought.

Local weather

Coastal and mountain areas often experience local variations in winds, temperature and rainfall, which seem to have no relation to the overall weather pattern of the larger area surrounding them. Cities also frequently have different types of weather from their surroundings (see page 34).

Land and sea breezes

Coastal areas often experience land and sea breezes, which form a local circulation of air affecting areas up to 30km (20 miles) inland. The breezes may blow in a different direction from the wind blowing across the rest of the country that day.

Land and sea surfaces heat up and cool down at different rates (see page 11). Sea breezes are formed on days of high pressure when the land heats up quickly. Air rises from the land forming a local area of relatively low pressure. This air spreads out as it meets high pressure air which is sinking. At the surface, air moves in from the sea to replace this rising air. This movement of air at the surface forms sea breezes.

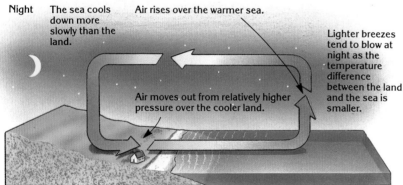

Day — Equal amounts of solar radiation fall on land and sea, but the land heats up more quickly.

High pressure air

Warm air rising, forming a local area of low pressure at the surface.

The air rises until it meets the high pressure air which is sinking.

The air spreads out over the sea, cools and sinks.

Sea breeze is formed as cooler air from over the sea moves in to replace rising air.

At night, the circulation is reversed as lower pressure forms over the warmer sea and air moves out from the land.

Night — The sea cools down more slowly than the land.

Air rises over the warmer sea.

Lighter breezes tend to blow at night as the temperature difference between the land and the sea is smaller.

Air moves out from relatively higher pressure over the cooler land.

Land and sea breezes do not form every day. For instance, on cloudy days, land and sea surfaces receive little solar radiation. This means that the temperature difference between the two surfaces is too small to start the circulation of air.

Coastal fog

Fog may be found at the coast, when there is sunshine only a short distance inland. Sea fog is formed when winds, blowing towards the coast from a warm source region, pass over the cold surface of the sea. The warm air is cooled below its dew point, forming fog (see page 15).

Water vapour in the warm air condenses to form fog over the sea as it is cooled to its dew point.

There is no fog inland as the land surface is warmer than the sea.

On-shore wind

Warm, humid air

Cold sea surface

At night, when the land cools down, the onshore winds may blow the fog further inland.

Ocean currents

Water travels around the world's oceans in currents, generally following the pattern of the prevailing winds which form them (see page 9). When a wind blows steadily in one direction for a long period, the moving air drags the surface of the water along, forming a current. The winds help to keep the currents moving in a steady flow.

Ocean currents can be either warm or cold, depending on where they were formed. They change the temperature of the air above them, bringing warm or cold air to places in their path.

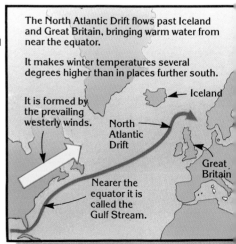

The North Atlantic Drift flows past Iceland and Great Britain, bringing warm water from near the equator.

It makes winter temperatures several degrees higher than in places further south.

It is formed by the prevailing westerly winds.

Iceland

North Atlantic Drift

Great Britain

Nearer the equator it is called the Gulf Stream.

Valley winds

Valleys often experience different weather from their surroundings. On clear, calm nights, for instance, fog often forms in valleys and light winds may blow down the mountain or hill slopes into the valley bottom. During the day, local winds may form which blow the other way, up the valley slopes.

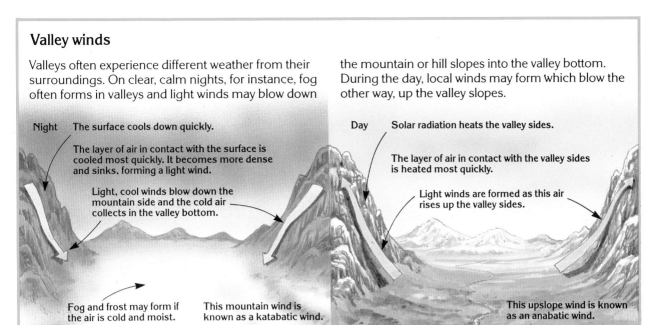

Night   The surface cools down quickly.

The layer of air in contact with the surface is cooled most quickly. It becomes more dense and sinks, forming a light wind.

Light, cool winds blow down the mountain side and the cold air collects in the valley bottom.

Fog and frost may form if the air is cold and moist.

This mountain wind is known as a katabatic wind.

Day   Solar radiation heats the valley sides.

The layer of air in contact with the valley sides is heated most quickly.

Light winds are formed as this air rises up the valley sides.

This upslope wind is known as an anabatic wind.

Rainbows

A rainbow is an isolated optical effect caused by the Sun's rays being refracted (bent) and reflected as they pass through millions of raindrops. For a rainbow to occur there needs to be bright sunshine and rain occurring at the same time.

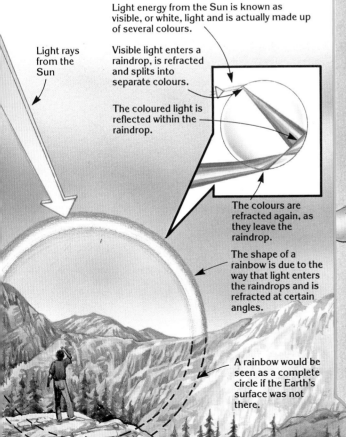

Light energy from the Sun is known as visible, or white, light and is actually made up of several colours.

Light rays from the Sun

Visible light enters a raindrop, is refracted and splits into separate colours.

The coloured light is reflected within the raindrop.

The colours are refracted again, as they leave the raindrop.

The shape of a rainbow is due to the way that light enters the raindrops and is refracted at certain angles.

A rainbow would be seen as a complete circle if the Earth's surface was not there.

A rainbow effect

It is possible to split the Sun's visible light into its separate colours, producing a rainbow effect. For this you will need a bowl of water, a piece of white cardboard, a small mirror and a very bright, sunny day.

What to do

1. Place the bowl of water in a very sunny position. Put the mirror into the bowl and lean it against the side.

Put a stone into the water to stop the mirror from slipping.

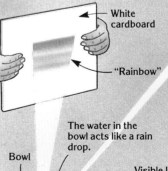

Mirror

Window

Bowl of water

White cardboard

"Rainbow"

2. Adjust the angle of the mirror so that a strong beam of sunshine falls on its surface. Move the cardboard around in front of the bowl, until a reflected "rainbow" appears on it.

The water in the bowl acts like a rain drop.

Bowl

Visible light is refracted as it enters the water.

It is then reflected by the mirror and refracted again as it leaves the water, producing a rainbow effect.

Monitoring the weather

In order to forecast the weather, meteorologists use information collected around the world. This information is based on observations made at the same time every day, at weather stations and elsewhere, using a variety of methods.

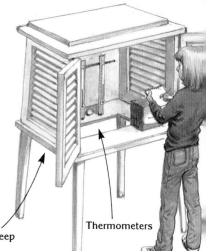

Weather stations

At weather stations, observers use a variety of instruments to monitor such things as wind speed, clouds, air temperature and pressure. They also record the general weather, such as if it is raining or foggy.

The methods and equipment used at every station are standardized, so the weather is monitored in exactly the same way.

Air temperatures are measured on the thermometers inside a Stevenson screen. The shuttered sides allow air to flow freely, but keep the thermometers out of direct sunlight.

Thermometers

Aircraft and ships

Many aircraft and ships provide weather information about areas where there are no weather stations. Like automatic weather stations on land (see below), they have equipment which records different weather conditions along their routes.

Many aircraft fly at an altitude of between 10-13km (30,000-40,000ft).

They provide useful information about high-level winds.

Ships provide information about weather conditions at sea.

This information is sent via satellite to a processing station on shore.

Automatic weather stations

Automatic weather stations are positioned in areas such as mountains or polar regions, where it would be difficult to have an observer permanently monitoring the weather. Computers are programmed to take readings from the weather instruments every hour.

An automatic weather station in Antarctica

Automatic stations are unable to provide information about cloud types, current weather conditions or visibility.

Radiosondes

The temperature, humidity and pressure at different heights above the ground are recorded by instruments called radiosondes. These are carried high into the air by balloons.

Balloon

The speed, direction and rate of ascent of the rising balloon indicate the strength and direction of the wind. As the balloon rises through the air, the temperature, humidity and pressure readings are taken by the radiosonde. Signals from radiosondes are transmitted to places called processing stations on the ground.

The balloon takes about an hour to rise to 20km (60,000ft).

It continues to rise until the pressure of the surrounding air becomes so low that the balloon bursts.

After it bursts, a small parachute opens and the radiosonde falls to the ground.

Radiosonde

Radiosondes are released from weather stations twice a day.

Many are lost, as they fall into the sea or land in remote areas. Some are returned to the weather stations by people who find them.

Weather satellites

Weather satellites provide essential information about the location and movement of weather systems, and the pattern of clouds around the Earth. Two types of weather satellite orbit the Earth.

Geostationary satellites orbit at a height of 36,000km (22,400 miles) above the equator.

Geostationary satellites orbit the Earth once every 24 hours, the same time the Earth takes to spin around its axis. This means that they always monitor the weather above the same place on the Earth's position.

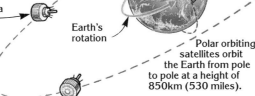

Polar orbiting satellite

Earth's rotation

Polar orbiting satellites orbit the Earth from pole to pole at a height of 850km (530 miles).

Polar orbiting satellites take about 100 minutes to complete one orbit, passing over both the Arctic and Antarctica. Each time they complete one orbit, the Earth has rotated by 25° longitude. This means a different strip of the Earth's surface is monitored on each orbit.

Satellite images

Weather satellites carry instruments called radiometers, which sense the intensity of reflected light or heat. This information is turned into images (pictures) at processing stations. The satellites are useful in locating and tracking the paths of weather systems, particularly over large oceans.

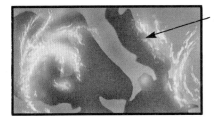

A visible satellite image

Different surfaces, such as cloud tops, land, water and ice reflect different amounts of sunlight. These different amounts show up as different shades of white or grey. These images cannot be produced at night as there is no light.

An infrared satellite image

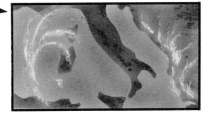

Infrared images are produced from measurements of heat, not light. The temperatures of different surfaces are recorded to produce these images. Infrared images of the Earth can be produced during the day and at night.

Radars

Weather radars are used to show where there is rain, hail or snow and how heavily they are falling. Radar systems work by sending out waves of radiation which bounce off rain drops and are reflected back, like echoes, to a receiving dish. The information is then sent, often via a satellite, to a processing station where it is turned into an image.

Radar images are colour-coded to show where the heaviest precipitation is occurring.

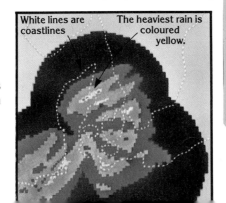

White lines are coastlines

The heaviest rain is coloured yellow.

A wind vane

All weather stations have a wind vane which indicates the direction of the wind. To make a wind vane you will need some thin cardboard, adhesive book covering film, 1m (40in) of 5mm (⅕in) dowel, glue, strong sticky tape, two cable clips and a pen lid.

What to do

1. Draw out the wind vane on the cardboard and cut it out. Cover one side with the film and score a line down the centre.

Cardboard

Covering film (for waterproofing)

12cm (4¾in)

8cm (3in)

25cm (9¾in)

3cm (1in)

12cm (4¾in)

2. Fold the vane in half. Stick the folded halves together (covered sides outwards) and cut across the narrow end to make a pointer. Use the tape to stick the pen lid to the vane.

Pen lid

Fold in half along the scored edge.

Pointer

3. Get someone to hold the dowel against a wooden post and attach it with the cable clips, so that the dowel does not turn.

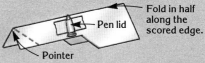

Place the vane on top of the dowel. Make sure it spins freely.

Wind

Dowel

Cable clips

4. Find reference points, such as trees or walls, for north, south, east and west, using a map or compass. The wind turns the vane until the pointer is pointing in the direction the wind is blowing from.

Remember, a wind is always named by the direction it blows from.

If the pointer is pointing to the east, the wind is blowing from east to west, so an easterly wind is blowing.

Your own weather station

Professional observers at weather stations around the world (see page 24) make regular observations to record weather conditions. By making daily observations and using simple equipment, you can set up your own weather station and begin a logbook to record your local weather.

Choosing a site

It is very important that the equipment used for recording different weather conditions is not affected by its surroundings. It is best to place the equipment in a relatively open area, such as a garden, but away from trees and tall buildings.

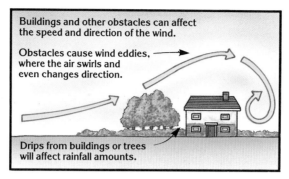

Buildings and other obstacles can affect the speed and direction of the wind.

Obstacles cause wind eddies, where the air swirls and even changes direction.

Drips from buildings or trees will affect rainfall amounts.

Temperature

Temperatures which are recorded at weather stations are taken in the shade (see page 24). You can make recordings by hanging a thermometer on a fence or a wall which is in the shade.

The highest and lowest temperatures can be recorded on maximum and minimum thermometers. You can buy these at a garden centre.

Minimum thermometer

Maximum thermometer

As the temperature rises or falls, the liquid in each thermometer moves an indicator. The indicator will remain at the highest (maximum thermometer) or the lowest (minimum thermometer) temperature reached.

Wind direction and speed

Wind direction is monitored on a wind vane (see page 25), which needs to be sited away from any obstacles. Wind speed is usually measured by an anemometer (but see below).

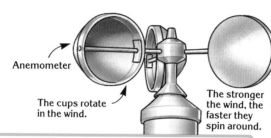

Anemometer

The cups rotate in the wind.

The stronger the wind, the faster they spin around.

Measuring wind speed

In order to measure wind speed at your weather station, you could make a simple wind box. You will need a shoe box, sticky tape, some thin cardboard, a knitting needle, a protractor, plastic film and a fine, permanent-ink pen.

What to do

1. Using the protractor and the permanent-ink pen, mark the angles for a wind-speed scale, at 5° intervals between 0° and 90° on the plastic film.

2. Cut the ends off the shoe box and lid, and stick them together. Cut a hole in one side of the box, near to one end (see below), and stick the scale inside, so it is displayed through the hole.

3. Push the knitting needle through the small, round hole (see previous picture), and wiggle it about until it rotates freely. Cut out a cardboard flap, slightly smaller than the end of the box. Stick it to the needle.

4. Hold the box so the flap faces into the wind. Look at the angle of the flap and work out the wind speed from the table below.

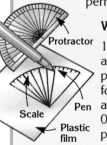

Protractor
Pen
Scale
Plastic film

Knitting needle
Flap

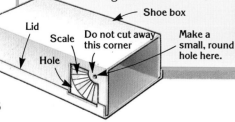

Lid
Scale
Hole
Do not cut away this corner
Shoe box
Make a small, round hole here.

Angle (°)	Km/h	Angle	Km/h
90	0	40	34-36
85	8-11	35	37-39
80	12-14	30	40-43
75	15-17	25	44-48
70	18-20	20	49-54
65	21-23		
60	24-25		
55	26-27	To convert km/h	
50	28-30	to mph, multiply	
45	31-33	by 0.621	

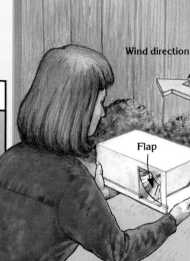

Wind direction

Flap

Visibility

Visibility is recorded as the distance a person can see. On a clear day, write down various landmarks you can see, such as a church or some hills. If your own weather station is in an area where the view is restricted, you could use a local open space to record the visibility. Use a map of your area (your local library should have one) to measure the distance from your recording point to each landmark.

Estimate the visibility by recording the furthest landmark you can see that day.

When visibility is less than 1km (3,000ft), it is said to be foggy.

Visibility is poor when you can see for between 1-5km (3,000ft-3 miles).

Clouds

Weather observers record the cloud types. They also record the cloud cover measured in oktas (see page 13).

Abbreviations are used to indicate each cloud type.

Cirrus – Ci
Cirrocumulus – Cc
Cirrostratus – Cs
Cumulus – Cu
Altocumulus – Ac

Stratus – St
Altostratus – As
Stratocumulus – Sc
Nimbostratus – Ns
Cumulonimbus – Cb

Visibility is said to be moderate when you can see for 5-10km (3-6 miles).

Visibility is said to be good when you can see for more than 10km (6 miles).

Pressure

Air pressure is measured on a barometer which should be placed inside a building. You can use your home-made barometer (see page 8) to record whether the pressure is rising or falling. You could also find out the exact pressure reading from your local weather centre.

The barometer should be placed away from direct sunlight. It should also be placed away from sources of heat, such as radiators and fires.

In your logbook, use arrows to indicate whether the pressure is rising or falling, or remaining the same.

Humidity

The humidity of the air is measured on wet and dry bulb thermometers (see page 21), which should be placed in the shade.

Precipitation

You can measure rainfall and other types of precipitation with your rain gauge (see page 15). Make sure it sits well away from trees and buildings.

Wet and dry bulb thermometers

A weather logbook

Try to take your observations at the same time each day. Start a logbook in which you can record all your readings. Also record the general weather, such as if it is raining or sunny. You could use the weather symbols on page 28 to record your observations.

Date	Time	Pressure Rising or Falling	Wind Speed	Wind Direction	Cloud Oktas	Cloud Type	Visibility	Temp	Humidity	Precipitation	General weather
1st Jan	08.00	↘	8-11 km/h	SW	8	Ns	poor	4°c	100%	2mm	rain
		→	12-14	W	8		poor	6°c	95%	0.5mm	drizzle

Analysing information

Weather observations, taken at weather stations all over the world (see page 24), are gathered together and distributed by special communication links to national weather centres in many countries, where all the information is analysed and weather maps are produced.

Incoming information

The information received at national weather centres includes observations made at manned and automatic weather stations, and on ships and aircraft, as well as information from processing stations, such as radiosonde readings, and satellite and radar images.

Some of these observations are turned into weather maps called synoptic charts, such as the one above right.

These use many different symbols to show the different readings. The key on the right shows the main symbols.

Every day, in addition to producing synoptic charts, the centres produce a computer model of the atmosphere (see page 29), based on the information they receive. After all their analyses are complete, they make the results available to those who need them.

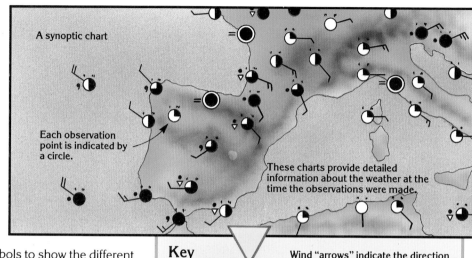

A synoptic chart

Each observation point is indicated by a circle.

These charts provide detailed information about the weather at the time the observations were made.

Key

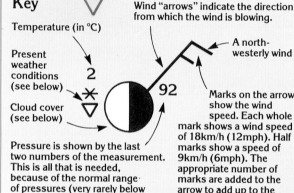

Temperature (in °C)

Present weather conditions (see below)

Cloud cover (see below)

Wind "arrows" indicate the direction from which the wind is blowing.

A north-westerly wind

Marks on the arrow show the wind speed. Each whole mark shows a wind speed of 18km/h (12mph). Half marks show a speed of 9km/h (6mph). The appropriate number of marks are added to the arrow to add up to the wind speed.

Pressure is shown by the last two numbers of the measurement. This is all that is needed, because of the normal range of pressures (very rarely below about 950mb or above 1040mb).

Cloud cover is measured in oktas (see page 13) and shown by the amount of the circle which is shaded. This shows there were 4 oktas of cloud. An extra white ring around the circle, and no wind arrow, means it was calm.

Key to symbols for weather conditions

Mist	=	Snow	✳
Fog	☰	Hail	▲
Rain	●	Thunderstorm	↯
Drizzle	,	The "showers" symbol is always shown with one, or more, other symbols:	
Showers	▽	Snow shower	✳/▽

Plotting observations

If you set up your own weather station (see pages 26-27), you could use the symbols shown on this page to show your own observations. Show the conditions for temperature, cloud cover, present weather, wind speed and direction.

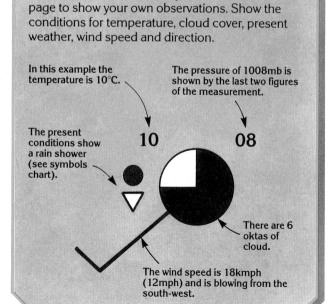

In this example the temperature is 10°C.

The pressure of 1008mb is shown by the last two figures of the measurement.

The present conditions show a rain shower (see symbols chart).

There are 6 oktas of cloud.

The wind speed is 18kmph (12mph) and is blowing from the south-west.

Computer models

Meteorologists use computers to predict what may happen to the weather for a period of time ahead. Using information from observations, calculations are made on computers to produce a model of the atmosphere as it was at the time when the observations were made. This model uses numbers to represent all the values for temperature, humidity, wind and pressure at different levels in the atmosphere.

Grid points

In order for the computer to predict what may happen to the atmosphere, all the different readings made at different levels have to be arranged in a regular pattern in the model. Imaginary lines of longitude and latitude divide the Earth's surface into a grid. The points where the lines meet are called grid points, and the readings are assigned to these points. In most cases, the actual observations were not made at places exactly on these grid points, but the readings are allotted to the grid point nearest to where they were made.

In areas where there is little or no information, the computer estimates conditions using readings from surrounding grid points and past information about the weather.

There are 40,000 imaginary grid points covering the Earth's surface.

The computer has readings for temperature, pressure, winds and humidity, not just for each grid point, but also for points at many levels directly above it.

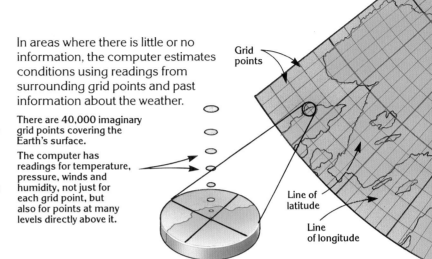

Grid points

Line of latitude

Line of longitude

Predictions

To make a prediction, the computer calculates changes that should occur to each set of grid point numbers in a short space of time ahead, usually ten minutes. This produces a new set of numbers for the computer to use. This "time-step" process is repeated many times, until the computer predicts, for instance, what the temperature and winds will be like twelve hours ahead. This whole process takes only a few minutes and then computer maps and charts are produced, based on the predictions, which weather forecasters can use.

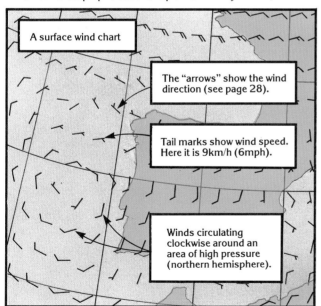

A surface wind chart

The "arrows" show the wind direction (see page 28).

Tail marks show wind speed. Here it is 9km/h (6mph).

Winds circulating clockwise around an area of high pressure (northern hemisphere).

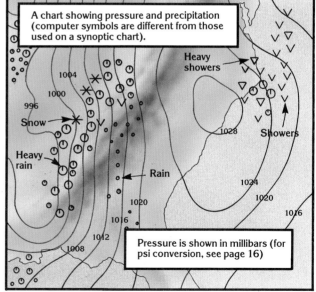

A chart showing pressure and precipitation (computer symbols are different from those used on a synoptic chart).

Heavy showers

Snow

Heavy rain

Rain

Showers

Pressure is shown in millibars (for psi conversion, see page 16)

Computer predictions about the weather twelve hours and twenty-four hours ahead are produced at national weather centres twice a day. The time-step process is usually continued to give predictions for up to a week ahead. These predictions may not be very accurate, however, because each time the time-step process is repeated, any small errors, which were present in the original grid point calculations, will reappear and become magnified. This is the reason why many long-term weather forecasts are often unreliable.

Weather forecasts

In order to predict the weather for the hours and days ahead, forecasters analyse information they receive from national weather centres (see pages 28-29). They look at the computer predictions but also use the observation maps and satellite images to make their own predictions. Forecasts reach the public via television, radio, newspapers and telephone information lines.

Weather forecasters

Weather forecasters work in many different places, such as the national weather centres themselves, or at separate city weather centres or meteorological offices at military and public airports.

They study all the information they receive and look closely for things such as fronts, highs and lows, which may bring a change to weather patterns. They also often add their knowledge of frequent local weather conditions, such as coastal fog (see page 22).

Forecasters at city weather centres have direct contact with some public services.

Severe weather conditions, such as fog, snow and ice greatly affect road transport.

When ice is expected, the relevant department can be alerted, so the roads can be sprayed with salt.

Television forecasts

Many weather forecasters on television are trained meteorologists. They make their own forecasts, using the large variety of information sent to them directly from a national weather centre. Other forecasters are television presenters who read out forecasts provided by a weather centre. The forecaster's predictions for the day ahead are presented as a sequence of weather maps, which have been drawn up on computers in the graphics department of the television centre. These weather maps may show, for example, temperatures, winds or a summary of the expected weather conditions. The forecasters also use "movies" (individual geostationary satellite images joined together) to show the movement of weather systems.

The maps (seen by the viewers) are changed by the forecaster, either with a hand-held remote control or by using certain "cue" words, as a sign for someone else to change the image.

During a weather broadcast, the forecaster stands in front of a blank screen, which is brightly coloured, for instance green.

The technique of changing background images is called colour separation overlay.

The studio camera films the forecaster and the screen.

The viewers see the forecaster and a series of weather maps on their screen, but the forecaster sees only the blank screen.

This is because, while the camera is filming, anything green is being replaced electronically by the computer weather maps.

Studio camera

The forecaster cannot wear any green clothes as they would "disappear" and the weather chart would appear in their place.

Radio and newspaper forecasts

Meteorologists at national and city weather centres provide radio stations and newspapers with information for their weather reports. National radio stations give a very generalized forecast for the whole country. Local radio stations, like local television stations, provide a more detailed forecast for their particular area. Newspaper forecasts are not as up-to-date, as the information they use has been issued at midday on the day before it appears in the newspaper.

Stormy conditions, such as high seas, create dangers for people who work at sea, so detailed advance warnings are needed. Some radio stations broadcast a specialized shipping forecast. These give warnings of severe weather conditions along with the expected wind speed and direction.

Up-to-date weather forecasts are particularly important for people who work at sea, e.g. on ships and oil rigs.

A meteorologist analysing satellite images, charts and maps.

A television monitor next to the camera shows the forecaster what the viewers are seeing, and helps him point to the correct places on the blank screen.

Who uses forecasts?

Weather forecasts are used by many specialized services, as well as being of interest to the public. Forecasts of approaching bad weather, such as storms or poor visibility, are of particular importance to aircraft, airports, shipping and fishing boats. Destinations can be changed, or routes diverted, to avoid bad weather conditions.

Specialized farming forecasts are broadcast on some television and radio stations. Farmers need to know if there is likely to be a severe frost, or if it is going to rain when they sow, harvest or spray their crops.

Farmers need to know when to spray crops with fertilizers or pesticides. If it rains within a few hours of the field being sprayed, the chemicals will be washed away and have no effect on the crops.

How accurate are forecasts?

Weather forecasters try to be as accurate as possible, but their predictions are not always correct. You could compare the forecasts given for your area, over a period of days. Make a chart for recording the accuracy of forecasts from newspaper, television, radio and telephone.

Record your own weather observations (see pages 26-27) and compare your records with the forecasts.

A forecast is fairly accurate if the wind speed is within 8km/h (5mph) and the temperature is within 2°C (4°F) of your readings.

Mark your chart with ticks or crosses depending on whether you think the forecast is accurate.

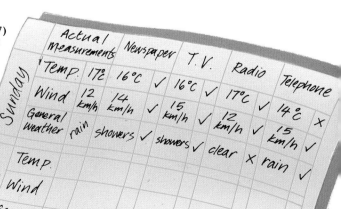

	Actual measurements	Newspaper		T.V.		Radio		Telephone	
Sunday Temp.	17°C	16°C	✓	16°C	✓	17°C	✓	14°C	✗
Wind	12 km/h	14 km/h	✓	15 km/h	✓	12 km/h	✓	15 km/h	✓
General weather	rain	showers	✓	showers	✓	clear	✗	rain	✓
Monday Temp.									
Wind									
General weather									

Worldwide climate

The climate of a particular area is the average pattern of weather which it experiences, measured over a long period. There are many different types of climate in different areas around the world, and these have a great effect on the vegetation and animals found there.

Climates around the world

World climates are classified into different types, mainly by latitude and temperature. Within each main type, variations may occur. For instance, coastal areas have maritime or mediterranean climates, whereas places in the centre of large continents have continental climates. When naming a climate, these variations are combined with the main types. For instance, a coastal area in the tropics has a tropical maritime climate.

The world's main climate types

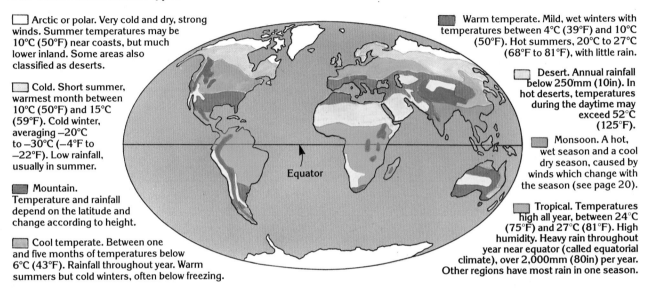

☐ Arctic or polar. Very cold and dry, strong winds. Summer temperatures may be 10°C (50°F) near coasts, but much lower inland. Some areas also classified as deserts.

☐ Cold. Short summer, warmest month between 10°C (50°F) and 15°C (59°F). Cold winter, averaging −20°C to −30°C (−4°F to −22°F). Low rainfall, usually in summer.

■ Mountain. Temperature and rainfall depend on the latitude and change according to height.

☐ Cool temperate. Between one and five months of temperatures below 6°C (43°F). Rainfall throughout year. Warm summers but cold winters, often below freezing.

Equator

■ Warm temperate. Mild, wet winters with temperatures between 4°C (39°F) and 10°C (50°F). Hot summers, 20°C to 27°C (68°F to 81°F), with little rain.

☐ Desert. Annual rainfall below 250mm (10in). In hot deserts, temperatures during the daytime may exceed 52°C (125°F).

■ Monsoon. A hot, wet season and a cool dry season, caused by winds which change with the season (see page 20).

■ Tropical. Temperatures high all year, between 24°C (75°F) and 27°C (81°F). High humidity. Heavy rain throughout year near equator (called equatorial climate), over 2,000mm (80in) per year. Other regions have most rain in one season.

Water loss from plants

Plants take in water through their roots and use it to make their food, but some water evaporates through tiny pores in their leaves.

To show that plants from different climates lose water vapour at different rates you need two 2 litre (2 quart) clear plastic bottles, a house plant, a cactus, two polythene bags, wire bag ties and plates, and some petroleum jelly.

What to do

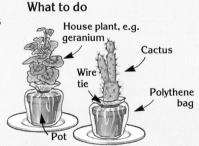

House plant, e.g. geranium
Cactus
Wire tie
Polythene bag
Pot

1. Give each plant 90ml (approx. 3 fl.oz) of water. Place each pot in a bag and fasten around the base of each plant with the wire ties. Place each plant on a plate.

2. Using a pair of scissors, carefully cut the base off each bottle.

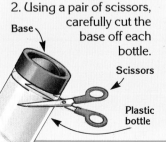

Base
Scissors
Plastic bottle

3. Place a bottle over each plant. Smear a thick layer of jelly around the base of each bottle.

Bottles (keep lids on)
Petroleum jelly
The jelly stops moisture from escaping.

Place each plate in a light, sunny position.

4. After three days, you should see water droplets on the inside of the bottles. These have condensed from water vapour given off by the plants.

Water droplets

More vapour should have been given off by the house plant.

The cactus comes from a desert where water is scarce. It loses very little water through its leaves (spines).

Climate and living things

Plants and animals are found in all areas of the world, each type adapted to the climate of its area. The fewest species are found where conditions are harshest, such as at the poles, and the greatest number in areas with much kinder climates. The most variety occurs in the warm, wet tropical areas.

Tropical rain forests

Rain forests are found in tropical areas near the equator, where there is over 2,000mm (80in) of rain a year. Temperatures are high, as, because of their position, these areas receive most solar energy (see page 6). Over half the Earth's species of plants and animals live in rain forests.

In tropical rain forests, it rains in short, heavy showers nearly every day. The warm, humid conditions provide the ideal living conditions for plants and animals.

Scarlet macaw

Surviving in deserts

In hot deserts, daytime temperatures are very high as there is hardly any cloud cover to protect the surface from the Sun's rays. It cools down quickly at night as heat radiates into space. There is little rain each year but fog and dew may form when the air cools at night. The few plants and animals which live in these regions have developed ways of surviving the intense heat and scarcity of water.

Ocelots hunt for their prey in forest trees and on the ground.

Some animals, such as the head-standing beetle, rely on fog or dew for water. The fog condenses on to its body, and it tilts forwards, so the droplets run into its mouth.

Many desert animals, including the head-standing beetle, escape the fierce heat by burrowing under the surface.

Many desert plants can store water in special cells when it rains. This means they can survive through the long, dry periods.

Leaf succulents have leaves which swell up to hold water.

Cacti store water in their stems. They also have spines instead of leaves. These have a much smaller surface area, so lose less water through evaporation.

Toucan

Squirrel monkey

Plants known as bromeliads grow on the trunks and branches of trees.

Red-eyed tree frogs live in the rainwater which collects in their leaves.

Surviving freezing temperatures

There are relatively few species of animals or plants living near the poles, where the temperature is nearly always below freezing.

In Antarctica, temperatures may fall below −40°C (−40°F).

Penguins are protected from the freezing temperatures by very dense feathers and a thick layer of fat under their skin.

Emerald tree boa

Giant armadillo

People and climate

People live in all the different climates of the world, ranging from the polar areas to the equator. In order to live a comfortable life, particularly where the climate is harsh, they have designed their houses, clothes and lifestyles to fit the conditions of their particular climate.

Building design

Most buildings are designed to make living in a particular climate as comfortable as possible. In temperate climates, with seasonal variations in temperature, many buildings have thick walls which trap the heat which builds up inside them. Many of these buildings are heated artificially in winter by fires and central heating. Windows are designed to let in maximum amounts of sunlight in winter and let out excess heat which builds up during the day in summer.

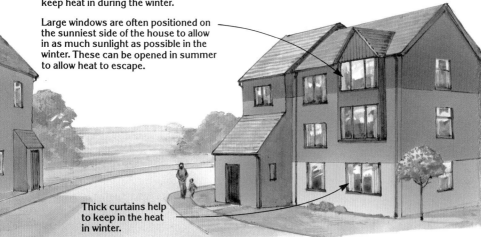

In temperate areas, houses are designed to keep heat in during the winter.

Large windows are often positioned on the sunniest side of the house to allow in as much sunlight as possible in the winter. These can be opened in summer to allow heat to escape.

Thick curtains help to keep in the heat in winter.

In hot climates, houses are designed for coolness. Most have few walls or partitions, to allow the maximum amount of air to circulate. Some buildings have window shutters, which are closed during the hottest part of the day, to keep the hot air out, and opened in the early morning and evening to allow cool air to circulate around the building.

In tropical areas, many houses have few inside walls. This allows air to circulate freely inside the building.

In areas of heavy rain, roofs are often built with a steep pitch (angle) to allow the water to drain off easily.

Houses are built on stilts in tropical areas to avoid being flooded during heavy rain.

City climates

Cities tend to have a different climate to their surrounding area because of their high concentration of buildings. They tend to be warmer at night, and may also get more rain in summer. The amount of pollution in the air also tends to be higher in cities (see page 40).

Tall buildings act as barriers to the wind. This either forces the wind upwards, or funnels it along the streets between buildings.

If the air rising over the city is exceptionally warm and humid, it may cool to form clouds, which may give short bursts of rain.

Building materials, such as bricks, stone and concrete, absorb a great deal of heat during the day.

At night, this heat is given off slowly, forming a "heat island", which makes a city up to 5°C (9°F) warmer than its surroundings.

Reflecting the Sun's heat

Different surfaces absorb and reflect different amounts of solar energy (see page 7). Light-coloured and shiny surfaces reflect the Sun's rays and so reduce the amount of heat which materials absorb.

In countries with a hot, sunny climate, buildings are often painted white, to reflect heat away. People also often wear light-coloured clothes to reduce the amount of heat their bodies receive.

In hot climates, buildings are white-washed to reflect the heat and help keep them cool.

People who live in extremely hot climates, such as deserts, wear long robes to protect them from the Sun and from wind-blown sand.

Just as few walls help air to move around inside a house, flowing robes help to circulate air around a body, keeping it cool.

The body and temperature

The human body reacts to different temperatures with various mechanisms which help it adjust its own temperature. Normally a person's body gives off heat, as it is warmer than the surrounding air. This heat is lost from the blood in blood vessels just under the surface of the skin.

When a person gets very hot, extra body heat is given off by sweating. As water evaporates from the skin, the body temperature is lowered. More heat is also lost from the skin's blood vessels, as these widen to allow more blood through.

When it is very cold, the blood vessels constrict, or become narrower, letting less blood through, so less heat is lost from the body. In extremely cold conditions, the supply of blood to some parts of the body, usually fingers and toes, may stop completely.

The blood travels into the surface blood vessels from the main arteries, and out of them via the veins.

The blood is pumped around all the blood vessels by the heart, and picks up heat as it travels.

Artery   Vein

If fingers and toes receive no blood, they receive no heat. The skin "dies". This is known as frostbite.

Making a radiometer

A radiometer is an instrument which uses reflection and absorption to measure solar energy. To make a simple radiometer, you need a black pen, a chewing gum wrapper, a jam jar, a pencil, some foil, strong glue, thread and a used matchstick.

What to do

Black surface
Chewing gum wrapper
Foil

◀ 1. Colour the paper side of the wrapper with the black pen. Cut it into four pieces, each 2cm x 2.5cm (¾in x 1in).

2. Stick the pieces of ▶ paper to one end of the matchstick (see right), with the shiny surfaces facing the same way.

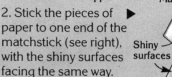

Matchstick
Shiny surfaces
Stick 12cm (5in) thread to the other end.

Pencil
Sticky tape
Thread
Jar
Radiometer

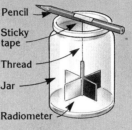

◀ 3. Wrap the loose end of thread around a pencil and secure it with some sticky tape. Suspend the radiometer in the jar.

4. Place the jar in a very sunny ▶ position.

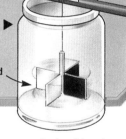

The radiometer turns as solar energy is absorbed by the black surfaces and reflected by the shiny surfaces.

Wind chill

The wind can make the air temperature feel colder than it actually is. This is called the wind chill factor. Normally, a thin layer of warm air surrounds your body, but if the wind is strong, this warm air is blown away, making you feel colder.

If the air temperature is 0°C (32°F) and a gentle breeze is blowing, the wind chill factor makes it feel like −3°C (27°F). If the wind speed increases to a strong breeze, the temperature feels like −10°C (14°F).

Scientists who work at the poles wear several layers of clothes to help insulate their body against freezing temperatures and the wind.

The clothes trap air which is warmed by the scientists' body heat, keeping them warm.

Changing climates

The Earth was formed about 4,600 million years ago, but the climate has not always been as it is today. At certain times, covering periods of thousands of years, it was much warmer than it is now. At other times, it was a lot colder, with much of the land covered in ice.

The first atmosphere

When the Earth was first formed, the atmosphere as we know it did not exist. The Earth's surface was a mass of liquid rocks which cooled to form a solid crust. As it cooled, the primitive atmosphere was formed from steam and poisonous gases, given off by erupting volcanoes.

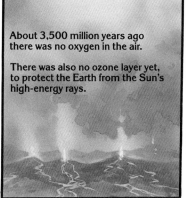

About 3,500 million years ago there was no oxygen in the air.

There was also no ozone layer yet, to protect the Earth from the Sun's high-energy rays.

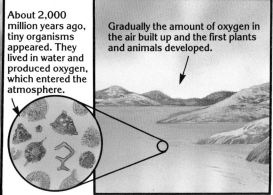

About 2,000 million years ago, tiny organisms appeared. They lived in water and produced oxygen, which entered the atmosphere.

Gradually the amount of oxygen in the air built up and the first plants and animals developed.

Ice ages

In the past, the Earth has gone through periods of time, called ice ages, when the climate was much colder and ice sheets covered huge areas of the surface. At the moment, ice sheets are found at the poles, but at times, ice has covered much larger areas.

Present-day ice sheet

Scientists think that ice ages have occurred about every 100,000 years and that they last for about 75,000 years. At the moment, the climate is between ice ages. This is called an interglacial climate.

Ice sheets are still found in the Arctic and Antarctic.

There are several theories which try to explain why ice ages occur. In the past, some scientists believed that the climate became colder because at certain times the amount of energy given off by the Sun decreased.

Ice ages have also been explained by a change in the Earth's angle of tilt on its axis and a change in the path of the Earth's orbit around the Sun.

The ice which forms the ice sheets has built up over thousands of years.

Climate change due to moving continents

The climate of each continent may have also changed because its position gradually changes. This is because the Earth's crust is made up of several pieces, called plates, which move very slowly, carrying the continents with them. Millions of years ago, many countries may have had a different climate because they were not found in the same latitude as they are today.

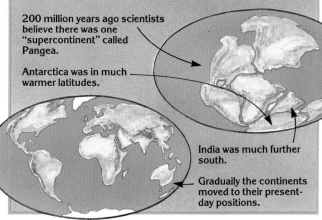

200 million years ago scientists believe there was one "supercontinent" called Pangea.

Antarctica was in much warmer latitudes.

India was much further south.

Gradually the continents moved to their present-day positions.

The Earth's present orbit around the Sun is almost a circle.

Over thousands of years the shape of the orbit may have gradually changed to an ellipse (oval) and back to a circle. This would have changed the amount of solar energy the Earth received. When the orbit changed to an ellipse, an ice age may have occurred as the Earth became cooler.

Volcanic eruptions

Scientists believe that erupting volcanoes may affect world climates. When a volcano erupts, fine volcanic dust may be thrown high into the atmosphere. The dust acts as a screen, reflecting more solar radiation back into space and preventing it from reaching the Earth.

It is thought that when the Earth was first formed, thousands of volcanoes covered the surface. Poisonous gases and dust, thrown out as the volcanoes erupted, greatly affected the climate.

Large volcanic eruptions still occur today, but they are very rare and their effect on the climate is short-term. Records show that the weather may be affected for two or three years following a huge eruption.

When Tambora in Indonesia erupted in 1815, volcanic dust was flung high into the atmosphere.

Dust from Tambora was spread around the world by high-level winds. Temperatures fell as the amount of solar radiation reaching the Earth decreased.

Climate change and the extinction of the dinosaurs

About 65 million years ago more than half the species of plant and animal life, including the dinosaurs, became extinct. Scientists believe that a sudden change in climate could have caused the mass extinction.

Dinosaurs existed on Earth for over 150 million years. During that time, the climate was believed to be warm and humid.

Some scientists believe that many species became extinct due to a massive volcanic eruption which blocked out the sunlight. This caused green plants to die, as they need sunlight to produce their food. In turn this meant many plant-eating animals died out.

Other scientists believe that a massive asteroid (immense rock in space), with a diameter of about 15km (9 miles), may have hit the Earth. The impact sent huge amounts of dust into the atmosphere, blocking out solar radiation.

Geological evidence

Most rocks are formed in layers, and by studying these layers, geologists (scientists who study rocks and their formation) are able to work out what the climate may have been like when each layer was formed.

Geologists use other methods to work out the age of the layers. By studying the minerals which make up a rock, they can date when rocks were formed. Once they have dated the layers, they can work out when climatic changes took place.

Rocks formed in warm climates contain a greater variety of fossils, compared with those formed in cooler times.

Rocks which lay at the surface during ice ages show evidence of being eroded, or worn away, by glaciers, or masses of moving ice.

Counting tree rings

Scientists work out climatic changes by studying the layers in rocks. In a similar way, by looking at the growth rings in the trunk of the tree which has fallen or died, it is possible to work out what the weather may have been like when it grew.

Each year the water-carrying tubes, or xylem, add new layers of cells in the centre of the tree's trunk, pushing the trunk outwards. In a year which has a warm, wet growing season more layers of cells will be added, producing a wide growth ring. In a season which has been dry or cold, the growth ring will be narrow.

You can work out the age of the tree by counting the rings.

A narrow growth ring shows that the growing season was cold and dry.

A wider growth ring indicates that the weather in that year was probably warm and wet.

This tree was 16 years old.

Present-day climate changes

At present, many scientists believe that world climates may be changing. They think this is due to the weather being affected by rising temperatures, caused by a build-up of certain gases in the atmosphere.

The greenhouse effect

The greenhouse effect is the term used to describe how the Earth is kept warm by heat trapped by gases in the lower atmosphere. It has been occurring for millions of years. Without the greenhouse effect, it is thought that the average temperature on the Earth's surface would be −15°C (5°F).

The gases, such as carbon dioxide and water vapour, are known as greenhouse gases, as they act like greenhouse glass. They let the Sun's high-energy radiation pass down through them to heat the Earth's surface, but absorb the lower energy radiation which the Earth sends back up. They then send out even lower energy in all directions. Some of this reaches the Earth, which receives extra heating.

High-energy radiation travels in through the glass of a greenhouse.

This is absorbed by the objects inside, which heat up. They send out lower energy radiation, which the glass absorbs.

The glass sends some radiation back, giving the objects extra heat.

In a similar way, the Earth's surface receives extra heating as greenhouse gases absorb and send out lower energy radiation.

Global warming

At present, average temperatures around the world are gradually rising. This is known as global warming. There could be a number of reasons for this, but many scientists link it with a known increase in greenhouse gases. They believe this has led to more heat being trapped, and that it is mainly due to man's activities.

The amount of carbon dioxide in the air has increased by 25% in the last hundred years.

Power stations and factories which burn fossil fuels (coal, oil and gas), give off carbon dioxide as they produce power.

Carbon dioxide is also given off as forests are cleared and burned, to make way for farmland and building.

The scientists believe that if the amount of greenhouse gases continues to rise at its present rate, average temperatures will increase by between 1.5°C and 4°C (3°F and 7°F) in the next fifty years. Many people agree with them, and are trying to reduce the amount of greenhouse gases released into the atmosphere.

Other greenhouse gases

Carbon dioxide and water vapour are the main greenhouse gases, but other gases, such as chlorofluorocarbons (CFC's), nitrous oxides and methane, also absorb out-going radiation. The amount of these gases is also increasing.

CFC's are given off by aerosol sprays and refrigerators.

CFC's are also thought to destroy ozone in the stratosphere (see page 40).

The effects of global warming

If world temperatures continued to rise, it would greatly affect world climates and the lives of people and wildlife.

There would be more rain in tropical areas, as the extra heat would increase the amount of water vapour in the air. Areas which receive little rain would receive even less, and turn into deserts, so people and animals would have to move away.

Sea temperatures would rise and this might lead to flooding in low-lying areas and an increase in the number of severe storms.

Nitrous oxides come from car exhaust fumes and from fertilizers used on fields.

Methane is given off from rotting vegetation and swamps. Growing rice in water-filled paddy fields to feed millions of people has meant creating man-made swamps which give off more methane.

Many animals kept for food give off methane as a waste gas.

The amount of rubbish people produce has increased. Methane is given off from rotting rubbish in refuse dumps.

If temperatures rose, many animals would not be able to adapt to the climate changes.

Many plants would die for lack of water, and animals would have to migrate, or move to other areas, in search of food and water.

If many plants die due to rising world temperatures, many species of animals could die out.

Rising sea levels

If world temperatures increase, sea levels may rise, for two main reasons. Firstly, when water is heated it becomes less dense and expands. If the sea temperature rose, its level would rise as the water expanded.

Secondly, higher temperatures could melt some of the ice which permanently covers some land, such as Antarctica and certain mountains. The water would eventually flow into the sea, making it rise. The melting of ice floating in the sea, however, would not add to rising sea levels.

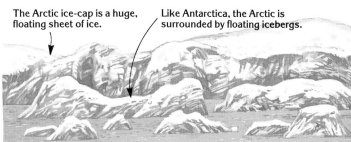

The Arctic ice-cap is a huge, floating sheet of ice.

Like Antarctica, the Arctic is surrounded by floating icebergs.

Even if all the ice in the Arctic melted, it would not cause a rise in sea levels. This is because when ice melts, the water which is left occupies less space than it did as ice.

Melting ice

The Arctic ice-cap floats on the sea. It would have little effect on the sea level if it melted. To carry out an experiment to show this, you need some ice cubes, a large glass bowl and a ruler.

What to do

1. Half-fill the bowl with water. Add ten ice cubes, and measure the water height.

Make sure all the ice cubes are floating in the water.

2. Wait for the ice cubes to melt.

3. Once the ice cubes have melted, measure the height of the water again.

The level of the water should be less than before the ice cubes melted. This is because the frozen water of the ice cubes took up more space. Now the cubes have melted, their volume as water is less than it was as ice.

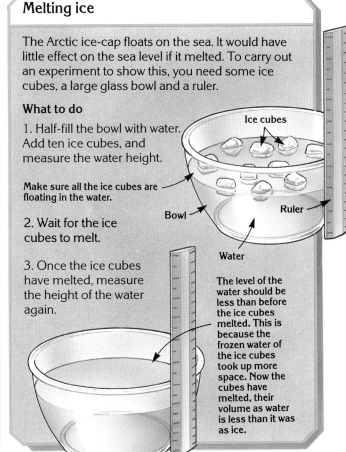

Ice cubes

Bowl

Ruler

Water

Pollution in the atmosphere

Air pollution is caused by any undesirable substance which enters the atmosphere and upsets the natural balance. These substances may be gases, liquids or solids, and are known as pollutants. Most pollutants are given off into the air as a result of human activities.

The ozone layer

Ozone is a gas, found throughout the Earth's atmosphere, but concentrated particularly in a layer in the stratosphere (see page 5). This layer is important because the molecules of gas stop harmful high-energy solar radiation from reaching the Earth's surface. Scientists have discovered that the ozone layer is getting thinner.

They think that substances in man-made gases called CFC's (see page 38) are rising into the stratosphere and breaking down the ozone molecules and that, if this continues, more and more harmful radiation will reach the Earth's surface. Exposure to harmful high-energy radiation can cause some forms of skin cancer.

Above Antarctica, scientists have discovered a "hole" where the ozone layer is thin.

They monitor the amount of ozone in the atmosphere using instruments attached to balloons.

Temperature inversions

In certain unusual conditions, a layer of warm air may trap colder air beneath it for several days at a time. This is called a temperature inversion.

When a temperature inversion occurs above a city, it greatly affects the build-up of pollutants, such as smog (smoke and fog). Normally, pollutants are dispersed, or scattered, through the atmosphere by moving air. The inversion prevents the air from rising, and traps the polluted air at a low level.

Warm air

Cooler air

Smog is formed as water condenses onto tiny particles, given off as fossil fuels are burned.

The air cannot rise as it is trapped beneath the warm air, so the pollution builds up.

Smog is not as common as it used to be. This is due to fewer buildings being heated by coal fires, and fewer power stations in cities.

Smog affects people with asthma and other breathing problems.

Surface ozone and photochemical smog

Some ozone, known as surface ozone, is found at ground level. It is a form of pollution and can cause health problems. It is formed by the chemical reaction of different pollutants with strong sunlight. The main pollutants in this case are nitrogen oxides and hydrocarbons from exhaust fumes.

When a large quantity of surface ozone builds up, it is known as photochemical smog. This is virtually invisible at street level, but can be seen as a brown haze hanging above a city.

Photochemical smog is an increasing problem in large cities in the summer.

Pollutant gases build up in the air at low levels and react with sunlight to produce surface ozone (photochemical smog). It causes people to suffer from eye irritations and sore throats.

Lead pollution

Lead is another air pollutant. It enters the air as particles from exhaust fumes, and is found much more in cities than in rural areas. Scientists believe that if people are exposed to large amounts of lead, it will build up in their blood and cause brain damage.

Lead-free petrol is now widely used to cut down on the amount of lead which pollutes the air.

Acid rain

Rainwater normally contains tiny amounts of acid, but this causes little damage. When mixed with some pollutants, though, it becomes much more acidic, and produces harmful rain known as acid rain.

Many animals cannot survive the higher acid levels, for example in lakes and rivers. Trees and other plants suffer as the acid makes them less resistant to frost and to attack by insects and diseases.

Acid rain also eats into and dissolves the surfaces it lands on, such as rocks. Harmful minerals are washed out of some rocks, and these do further damage to animals and plants (see picture, below).

Pollutants such as sulphur dioxide and nitrous oxide make rainwater more acidic. They enter the air in exhaust fumes, and when fossil fuels are burned.

Acid rain clouds may be blown for long distances before the rain falls.

Acid rain falls.

Harmful minerals, such as aluminium, are washed into rivers and lakes from dissolved rocks.

High concentrations of some minerals can affect plants and animals.

Aluminium reduces the amount of oxygen which fish can absorb through their gills, eventually causing them to die.

The pollutants mix with water vapour and a chemical reaction occurs, producing droplets of sulphuric and nitric acid.

Aluminium from dissolved rocks affects plant roots, stopping them absorbing other, essential minerals.

In some of the worst-affected areas, there are no fish left in rivers and whole forests have been killed.

Acid rain indicator

Most rainwater is slightly acidic. To make an indicator to see how acidic your rain is, compared with other substances, you need some red cabbage, white vinegar, bicarbonate of soda, a jug and some jars.

What to do

1. Collect some rainwater in a jar. Chop up 3 large cabbage leaves. Put them into a saucepan with ½l (1 pint) of tap water. Boil them gently for ten minutes.

2. Let the mixture cool, then pour the liquid through a sieve into the jug.

3. Test your indicator liquid by pouring 1cm (½in) depth into two jars. Add a few drops of vinegar to one and ½tsp of bicarbonate to the other.

4. In the same way, use your indicator to test some rainwater to see how acidic it is.

The pinker the indicator, the more acidic the substance being added to it.

Red cabbage leaves

Sieve

Teaspoon

Vinegar

Bicarbonate of soda

Blue/purple liquid (indicator liquid)

Bicarbonate is an alkali and should turn the indicator green.

Vinegar is an acid and should turn it pink.

The jar with vinegar added can be used as a comparison.

Rainwater

Predicting future weather

With the current concern about global warming (see page 38), meteorologists are trying to predict what effect rising temperatures may have on weather and climates around the world in the future. They use computer models to work out future climates, in a similar way to forecasting daily weather (see page 29).

General circulation models

Scientists use computer models, called general circulation models, or GCM's, to predict future weather patterns. Their computers contain vast amounts of information, about the atmosphere, such as its composition of gases, average surface and upper air temperatures and humidity, as well as information about oceans.

By changing particular pieces of information, for instance by adding more greenhouse gases, scientists can create new models which show what effect global warming may have on weather in the future.

GCM's have predicted that in continental regions, such as in North America, rainfall may increase in winter and temperatures may rise by 2-4°C (4-7°F) in the next fifty years.

There could also be a 2-3°C (3-5°F) temperature rise in summer, with less rain.

This change in climate could greatly affect the amount of wheat which is grown in the vast areas of North America, known as the prairies.

Uneven temperature increases

Using general circulation models, scientists have predicted that there may be an average temperature rise of 1.5°C (2.7°F) by the year 2050. They think that temperatures will rise unevenly, though, with the greatest rise at the poles. This will have an increase of up to 4°C (7°F), compared to 1°C (1.8°F) in tropical areas.

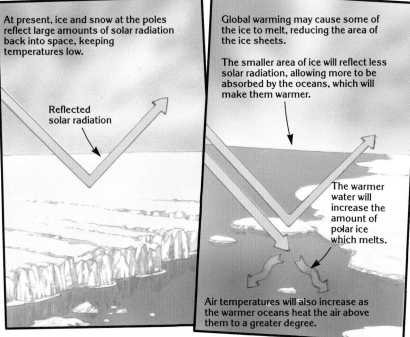

At present, ice and snow at the poles reflect large amounts of solar radiation back into space, keeping temperatures low.

Reflected solar radiation

Global warming may cause some of the ice to melt, reducing the area of the ice sheets.

The smaller area of ice will reflect less solar radiation, allowing more to be absorbed by the oceans, which will make them warmer.

The warmer water will increase the amount of polar ice which melts.

Air temperatures will also increase as the warmer oceans heat the air above them to a greater degree.

Predicted temperature increases around the world

Equator

■ Over 4°C (7°F)	□ 2-2.5°C (3.5-4.5°F)	The predicted rises in temperature may change the pattern of climates around the world (see page 32).
■ 3.5-4°C (6-7°F)	□ Less than 2°C (3.5°C)	
□ 2.5-3.5°C (4.5-6°F)		

Changing cloud cover

Some scientists believe that in a warmer world there would be more clouds, as greater amounts of water would evaporate from seas. This could lead to many areas having more rain than they do now. Also, some types of cloud reflect solar radiation, while others absorb radiation from the Earth's surface. Depending on the type and amount of "new" cloud, the rate at which global warming occurs could be affected.

If the number of clouds increases, the rate of global warming may be reduced, or even halted, but it may also be increased. Whether temperatures increase or decrease may depend on the type of clouds which are formed.

More storms?

Some scientists believe that extreme weather conditions, such as storms, hurricanes and floods could become more frequent in a warmer world, particularly in tropical areas. Even though the temperature increase in tropical areas may be small, the warmer temperatures could lead to more hurricanes, as there would be a greater area of sea with temperatures above 27°C (80°F) (see page 18).

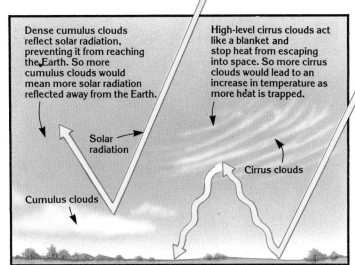

Dense cumulus clouds reflect solar radiation, preventing it from reaching the Earth. So more cumulus clouds would mean more solar radiation reflected away from the Earth.

High-level cirrus clouds act like a blanket and stop heat from escaping into space. So more cirrus clouds would lead to an increase in temperature as more heat is trapped.

Solar radiation

Cirrus clouds

Cumulus clouds

Hurricane winds produce massive waves, called storm surges.

As a hurricane approaches land, waves crash on to land causing damage and severe flooding.

If there are more hurricanes, low-lying areas already at risk from rising sea levels may also suffer from more storm surges.

In 1991, the coast of Bangladesh was hit by a storm surge which killed thousands of people.

Other scientists believe that storms could become less frequent, particularly in temperate areas. Areas of low pressure, which lead to storms, develop because of the large temperature difference between polar and tropical air (see page 16). Due to the predicted uneven increase in world temperatures, this difference would become smaller, so, according to these scientists, fewer severe storms would occur.

A bottle hurricane

Winds within a hurricane rise in a spiral motion, known as a vortex. It is possible to create your own vortex in a bottle. For this you will need two identical clear plastic bottles (also with plastic tops), some very strong glue and a corkscrew.

What to do

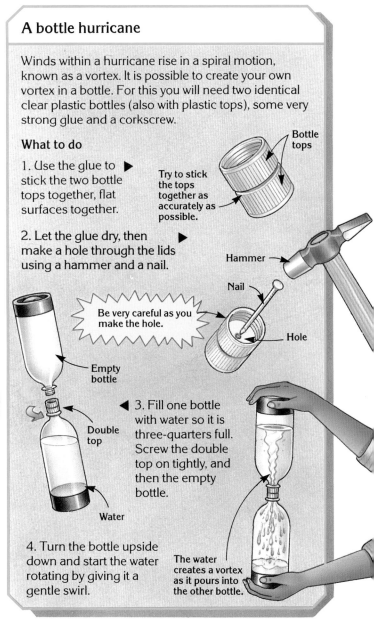

1. Use the glue to stick the two bottle tops together, flat surfaces together.

Try to stick the tops together as accurately as possible.

Bottle tops

2. Let the glue dry, then make a hole through the lids using a hammer and a nail.

Hammer

Nail

Be very careful as you make the hole.

Hole

Empty bottle

3. Fill one bottle with water so it is three-quarters full. Screw the double top on tightly, and then the empty bottle.

Double top

Water

4. Turn the bottle upside down and start the water rotating by giving it a gentle swirl.

The water creates a vortex as it pours into the other bottle.

Record weather extremes

Record-breaking weather and climate conditions have been monitored by meteorologists all around the world.

The rainiest climate

The wettest place in the world, with the highest number of rainy days each year, is Mt. Wai-'ale-'ale on the island of Kauai in Hawaii. It rains on as many as 350 days each year.

The Hawaiian islands lie in the Pacific Ocean. The south-east trade winds blow here, all year. These winds are warm and moist.

The winds cool as they are forced to rise over Mt. Wai-'ale-'ale.

Dense clouds form and heavy rain falls on the windward side of the mountain.

The average annual rainfall here is 11,455mm (451in).

By contrast, places on the leeward side, or sheltered side, of the mountains receive as little as 250mm (10in) each year. This is because the winds are warmed as they descend, and contain less water vapour.

Places on the sheltered side are said to be in a rain shadow.

Longest drought

The driest place in the world, which has also experienced the longest drought, is Calama in the Atacama Desert in Chile. It is said that up until 1971 there had been no rain there for 400 years.

The Atacama Desert receives very little rain because it lies in the rain shadow of the Andes mountain range.

Equator (0°)

Atacama Desert

The south-east trade winds lose their moisture as they rise over the Andes.

Andes Mountains

As well as being in a rain shadow, the Atacama Desert is dry because it lies in the high pressure band around latitudes 30°S (see page 9), so the air is sinking.

Any warm thermals (see page 7) cannot rise very far due to the sinking air, so no clouds are formed.

30°S

Hottest climate

Dallol in Ethopia, on the eastern edge of the Sahara Desert, has an average annual temperature of 34.4°C (93.9°F), making it the hottest place in the world.

Clouds greatly affect the amount of solar radiation which reaches the Earth's surface (see page 43).

Few clouds are found above the Sahara Desert, which lies in the band of permanent high pressure at roughly 30°N (see page 8).

Here, air from tropical regions further south sinks towards the Earth's surface.

The air becomes warmer as it sinks, so any water vapour it contains does not condense to form clouds.

The hot surface greatly heats the air above it.

The highest air temperature ever recorded was at Al 'Aziziyah in Libya, which is also at the edge of the Sahara Desert. The temperature reached 58°C (136.4°F) in the shade (meterologists always measure temperatures in the shade – see page 24).

Coldest climate

The coldest climate in the world is in Antarctica. Scientists at the Plateau research station in Antarctica have kept records which show the average annual temperature to be −56.6°C (−69.8°F).

The lowest air temperature was also recorded in Antarctica, at the Russian research station in Vostok. The temperature fell to −89.2°C (−128.6°F).

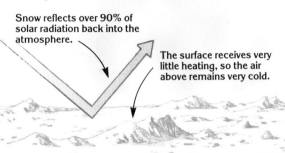

Snow reflects over 90% of solar radiation back into the atmosphere.

The surface receives very little heating, so the air above remains very cold.

The lowest number of hours of sunshine is also found at the south pole. The Sun does not rise for 182 days each year, due to the tilt of the Earth (see page 6).

Air pressure and wind speed

The highest recorded air pressure occurred in Agata, in northern Siberia. The pressure of the air at sea level reached 1083.8mb (32 psi).

The lowest air pressure, which measured 870mb (25.69 psi), was recorded in the centre of Typhoon (hurricane) Tip which occurred above the Pacific Ocean in 1979. A U.S. Air Force aircraft flew into the eye of the hurricane (see page 19) to measure the pressure.

The highest recorded surface wind speed of 450km/h (280mph) was caused by a tornado in Texas, USA.

The lowest pressure which occurs may never be measured as it will probably occur at the very centre of a tornado (see page 47).

It is unlikely that a barometer could be positioned at exactly the right place to measure the pressure.

It is also unlikely that any instrument would survive the incredibly strong winds caused by tornados.

Observing wind speed

The speed of the wind is usually measured on an anemometer, but it can be estimated using a scale called the Beaufort scale. The scale is based on the effect of the wind at different speeds.

Force — Description — Speed

0. Calm. Smoke rises vertically.

0km/h (0mph)

1. Light wind. Wind direction shown by smoke.

1-5km/h (1-3mph)

2. Light breeze. Wind felt on face, leaves rustle.

6-11km/h (4-7mph)

3. Gentle breeze. Leaves and twigs constantly move, flags begin to flutter.

12-19km/h (8-12mph)

4. Moderate breeze. Dust and paper blown about, small branches on trees move.

20-29km/h (13-18mph)

5. Fresh breeze. Small trees sway, small waves on lakes.

30-39km/h (19-24mph)

6. Strong breeze. Large branches on trees move, difficult to use an umbrella.

40-50km/h (25-31mph)

7. Near gale force. Whole trees sway, difficult to walk against the wind.

51-61km/h (32-38mph)

8. Gale. Twigs broken off trees, very difficult to walk.

62-74km/h (39-46mph)

9. Severe gale. Chimney pots and roof tiles break off.

75-87km/h (47-54mph)

10. Storm. Seldom occurs away from coasts, trees uprooted, buildings damaged.

88-101km/h (55-63mph)

11. Violent storm. Very rarely occurs, widespread damage.

102-117km/h (64-73mph)

12. Hurricane. Total devastation.

118+km/h (74+mph)

Glossary

Acid rain. Rain which contains water droplets that have absorbed pollutants from the atmosphere and become unusually acidic. The term is also used to describe dry pollutants which fall on to surfaces from the air.

Anemometer. An instrument used for measuring the speed of the wind. ▼

Anticyclone. An area of relatively high air pressure, also known as a high.

Atmospheric pressure (air pressure). The weight of air pushing down on a planet's surface.

Barometer. An instrument which measures air pressure.

Beaufort scale. A scale used for measuring the strength of the wind, based on observations.

Blocking high. A high pressure area which remains stationary and diverts the normal path of lows across an area of the Earth's surface.

Climate. The weather conditions experienced in an area over a long period.

Cold front. The boundary between a mass of cold air and a mass of warmer air where the cold air is moving in to replace the warmer air.

Computer model. A representation of the atmosphere created by a computer, used by meteorologists to produce a weather forecast.

Condensation. A process by which a gas or vapour changes into a liquid.

Convection. The upward movement of air which has been heated by the land or sea surface below.

Coriolis effect. The effect caused by the Earth's rotation which appears to deflect air as it moves between two places.

Cyclone. An area of low pressure. It may also be called a low or a depression.

Dew point. The temperature at which water vapour condenses to form water.

Evaporation. A process by which a liquid changes into a gas or vapour.

Front. The boundary that separates two masses of air of different temperature.

Geostationary satellite. A weather satellite which stays above the same place on the Earth's surface.

Global warming. An overall increase in world temperatures which may be caused by additional heat being trapped by greenhouse gases, such as carbon dioxide and CFC's.

Greenhouse effect. The heating effect caused by gases in the atmosphere trapping heat (radiation) from the Earth's surface.

Humidity. The amount of water vapour in the air.

Ice ages. Periods of time when ice covered large areas of the Earth's surface.

Intertropical Convergence Zone (ITCZ). A band of low pressure, formed around the equator, where warm air ▼ rises and is replaced by air moving in from the northern and southern hemispheres.

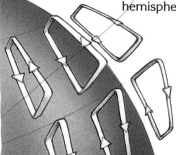

Isobar. A line on a weather map joining places which have equal atmospheric, or air, pressure.

Jet stream. The strongest currents of the high-level winds which circle the Earth between 10km and 16km (6 miles and 10 miles) above the surface.

Meteorologist. A scientist who studies all the elements of the atmosphere which combine to form the weather.

Monsoon. A wind which blows from different directions at different times of the year, creating a wet, or rainy season, and a dry season.

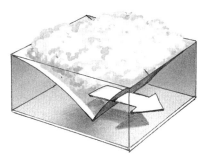

Occluded front. A front which occurs where a cold front moves in and undercuts a warm front, lifting the warm air away from the surface.

Ozone layer. A layer of ozone gas, found in the upper atmosphere, which absorbs harmful solar radiation.

Polar front. The boundary where cool air moving in from polar regions meets warm tropical air.

Polar orbiting satellite. A weather satellite which travels over both the north and south poles each time it completes one orbit of the Earth.

Precipitation. Any form of moisture, such as rain, snow, sleet or hail, that falls to the ground from a cloud.

Prevailing wind. The most common wind which tends to blow in any given location.

Radiosonde. An instrument, attached to a balloon, which monitors pressure, temperature and humidity at different heights above the Earth's surface.

Smog. Fog mixed with air pollutants, such as smoke, which cause the fog to become more dense.

Solar radiation. Heat and light energy from the Sun.

Synoptic chart. A chart which shows various elements of the weather, such as temperature and pressure, monitored in different places at the same time.

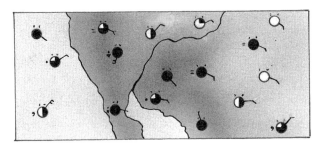

Temperature inversion. A situation which arises where a layer of warmer air lies above cooler air, making the temperature increase or stay the same, rather than decreasing, with height.

Thermal. A rising current of warm air which is caused by a local area of the Earth's surface heating up more than its surroundings.

Tornado. A violently rotating column of air which may extend from the base of a cumulonimbus cloud. It is thought to be formed by strong upward currents of air which exist within the cloud.

Tropical cyclone. A severe storm, with torrential rain and strong winds, formed over warm seas between 5° and 20° north and south of the equator. It may also be called a hurricane or a typhoon.

Warm front. The boundary between a mass of warm air and a mass of cooler air, where the warm air moves in to replace the cooler air.

Wind. Air moving from high pressure areas to areas of lower pressure.

Index